TASTE OF INDONESIA

Taste of
INDONESIA

OVER 70 AROMATIC DISHES FROM THE
SPICE ISLANDS OF BALI, JAVA,
SUMATRA AND MADURA

SALLIE MORRIS

SMITHMARK

© 1996 Anness Publishing Limited

This edition published in 1996
by SMITHMARK Publishers, a division of US Media Holdings, Inc.
16 East 32nd Street
New York
NY 10016

SMITHMARK Books are available for bulk purchase
for sales promotion and for premium use. For details write or call the Manager
of Special Sales, SMITHMARK Publishers,
16 East 32nd Street, New York, NY 10016; (212) 532-6600

Produced by Anness Publishing Limited
1 Boundary Row
London SE1 8HP

ISBN 1 8317-7402-9

Publisher: Joanna Lorenz
Senior Cookery Editor: Linda Fraser
Cookery Editor: Anne Hildyard
Copy Editor: Val Barrett
Designer: Siân Keogh
Photography and styling: Patrick McLeavey, assisted by Jo Brewer
Food for Photography: Jane Stevenson assisted by Lucy McElvie
Illustrator: Madeleine David

Printed in Singapore by Star Standard Industries Pte. Ltd.

CONTENTS

Introduction 6

Soups and Snacks *12*

Fish and Seafood *30*

Meat and Poultry *42*

Sambals and Pickles *58*

Rice and Noodles *68*

Vegetables and Salads *78*

Desserts *90*

Index *96*

INTRODUCTION

Visitors to Indonesia might be able to name just a handful of the more widely known and frequently visited islands, such as Bali, Java, Lombok and Sumatra, which are part of the fabled Spice-Island archipelago.

They may be surprised to know that the population of Indonesia now exceeds 185 million and is still growing. What is more surprising is that only 4,000 of the 17,000 islands are inhabited.

Over the centuries, waves of traders and merchants landed on Indonesia, in search of valuable spices from these lush tropical and volcanic islands. They left behind influences on the culture, religion, customs and, of course, cuisine. Indonesian food cleverly accommodates this rich tapestry of foods brought by migrants and traders over the centuries and today we can enjoy the delicious kaleidoscope of tastes, textures and warm, spicy aromas of this fascinating cuisine.

Hindus in the first century and Buddhists in the eighth century left a legacy of vegetarianism, along with many beautiful temples; the most famous is the world's largest, at Borabodur, near Jogjakarta, in central Java. Islam was brought to the islands by Arab traders in the fifteenth century and is the faith embraced by 85 per cent of Indonesians today. This should mean that pork is off limits but there are islands, such as Bali, where pork is elevated to festival food – and Bali has a lot of festivals, as we discovered on one of our visits there.

The next traders after the Arabs were the Portuguese, followed by the Dutch, who stayed for 250 years, until Independence in 1945. In addition, a steady flow of Chinese migrant traders, merchants and workers over the centuries gave another dimension to the richness of Indonesian cuisine and its warm and generous people.

Sir Stamford Raffles, founder of Singapore and a one-time resident, wrote "By the custom of the country, good food and lodging are ordered to be provided for all strangers and travelers arriving at a village and in no country are the rights of hospitality more strictly observed by both custom and practice."

Rice is the staple food and it grows in abundance throughout the islands. The view from the air over Java was of hundreds of miles in any direction of lush green paddy fields. Driving along country roads on Bali – they are all "country" roads on this most exquisite island – we were captivated by the view as we rounded each corner: terraces of paddies, fringed with palm trees, which, away from the south-coast area of serious tourism called Kuta, had us almost believing that this was a little glimpse of heaven. On Madura, another island just north of

Exotic fruit and vegetables are the order of the day at this colorful outdoor market in Denpasar, on the beautiful Indonesian island of Bali.

Java, we spent a delightful sojourn. There, we had home-cooking at its best and I left the island with photographs and recipes which greatly enhanced and extended my knowledge of Indonesian cuisine.

Madura, unlike its neighbor Java, is about the same size as England, but it is rather dry and almost arid. Lack of rainfall is a problem; where other islands always get two and possibly three crops of rice, Madura gets one certain crop and, if lucky, enough rain just to sustain the second crop. The island has not as yet been "discovered" by tourism, though the bull races held during August and September rival those through any Spanish town. Heats are held in each district, with the final being held in Pamekasan in September. The bulls are specially fed on beer, eggs and chilies, which may account for their 30mph speeds over the 100 metre course!

Though there are many people throughout this vast country only just managing to get by, feast days and festivals, where food plays an important and vital part, abound. Along all the roads in Bali are little temples, where daily offerings of fruit and flowers are made to the gods. The Balinese have an inner faith and grace that seems to transcend the trappings of tourism. It is rare to meet anyone who has been there who would not like to return to this Garden of Eden.

Eating out is easy in the warm tropical climate. People seem to eat all the time! Padang restaurants are popular, with a vast choice of dishes. We were always very impressed by the waiters, who carry up to ten different plates of food to your table, balanced cleverly on their arms. In Padang restaurants, you help yourself, then the plates are cleared away and you only pay for what you have eaten!

A buffet-style meal makes sense when serving Indonesian food. Guests put a few spoonfuls of rice in wide-brimmed soup plates, moisten them

At an early morning market at Nusa Penida, on the island of Bali, shoppers are buying small, silvery fish on bamboo skewers, ready for the barbecue.

with one of the soups, usually a *sayur*, and then put spoonfuls of whatever they fancy from the dishes on offer individually round the edge of the plate. The dish is topped with perhaps a few crisp deep-fried onions, a spot of chili sambal and a crisp shrimp cracker, to complete the full range of textures and flavors that make up a truly memorable Indonesian meal.

For a lavish spread for 8–10 people, the following would be a suitable selection of dishes:

Vegetable Broth with Ground Beef
Rendang
Spicy Squid
Festive Rice
Corn Fritters
Sweet and Sour Fruit and Vegetable Salad
Steamed Coconut Custard

This meal would typically be eaten with a spoon and fork. Usually, soft drinks, or possibly beer are served with such a meal.

Selemat makan "Good eating," as they say in Indonesia.

INGREDIENTS

BANANA LEAVES
Banana leaves are used as the South-east Asian answer to aluminum foil and are available at some Asian stores in the US. Make the leaves more pliable by plunging them into boiling water or holding them over a flame, before placing the ingredients for cooking inside. Make into a neat package and secure with a saté stick or a fine skewer. Food wrapped in this way is sometimes steamed and frequently broiled and gains flavor from the banana leaf itself.

BANGKUANG (yambean)
These are the same shape as a turnip but with a smooth, light golden skin, which should be thinly peeled. The texture is somewhere between an apple and a hard pear. Peel and cut in julienne strips, to use in stir-fries, spring rolls or salads.

BEAN CURD (tofu)
Sold in the refrigerated section in Asian stores and many supermarkets, these fragile looking 3-inch cubes are available fresh. They are made from soybean milk set with gypsum and are popular with vegetarians. In spite of its bland flavor, bean curd is full of protein. It will keep in the fridge for 3–4 days, if covered with fresh water daily. A long-life version is available; once opened, use it as fresh

Clockwise from left: black rice, bean thread cellophane noodles and dried egg noodles.

Clockwise from top: large purple eggplants, garden eggs and small yellow eggplants.

and store as directed on the package.

Tempe is made from whole fermented soybeans, to give a cake which is bursting with protein, plus iron and vitamin B. Cut into cubes or slices and add to dishes as directed on the package.

BEAN SPROUTS
Readily available at vegetable markets and supermarkets. Chill in the package and use as soon as possible. Most sprouted beans come from mung beans, though soybeans are also available. Both can be sprouted at home.

CHILIES
Available from most markets, the chili is grown on a dwarf bush with small dense green leaves, white flowers and red or green finger-shaped fruit. There are so many varieties of fresh chili peppers now available that books are written describing and differentiating between them. From largest to smallest, some of the more frequently found are cayenne, sevano, jalapeño, habañeros, and bird peppers. The last two are fiercely hot. In general, the green chili is less hot and has a rather earthy heat; the red is usually hotter and sometimes very fiery. To prepare, remove the cap from the stalk end and slit it from top to bottom with a small knife. Under

running water, scoop out the seeds (unless you like food fiercely hot) with the knife point. Use rubber gloves or wash your hands thoroughly with soap and water. Use the recipe for Chili Sambal, if you have a plentiful supply of chilies, or buy the jars of chopped fresh chili available at specialty Asian stores. After opening, keep the chilies in the fridge.

COCONUT MILK AND CREAM
In South-east Asia, the canned variety is often used, simply for convenience. (The liquid inside a whole coconut is coconut juice and not coconut milk – it makes a refreshing drink when chilled.) Once opened, chill canned milk for 4–5 days or freeze it.

Coconut cream can sometimes be found in Asian markets, frozen or refrigerated.

Instant powdered coconut milk is widely available. Packages of frozen coconut milk are available too.

Dried coconut is a very successful way of obtaining good-quality coconut milk and cream. Buy unsweetened coconut; larger and cheaper quantities can be bought in Asian supermarkets. Empty 1 cup into a food processor with 2 cups boiling water. Process for 20–30 seconds and set aside to cool. If making several batches, empty each lot into a large bowl after processing and

Clockwise from left: Coconut shells with the meat removed, whole fresh coconut and coconut cream.

Clockwise from left: fresh ginger root, fresh galangal roots and fresh turmeric roots, cut to show their vivid color.

allow to cool. Place a large strainer over a large bowl and line it with cheesecloth or a dish towel. Ladle some of the cooled mixture into the cloth, fold the edges over the coconut and twist the ends, to squeeze out the maximum amount of milk. Repeat with the remaining coconut. You can use the squeezed coconut to make a second batch, but it will not be as rich.

CORIANDER
Available all over South-east Asia, the seeds are more often used than the leaves in Indonesian cuisine. The flavor is greatly enhanced by dry-frying.

DUAN SALAM LEAVES
Only available dried, these resemble bay leaves, which are a good substitute if duan salam leaves are hard to find. Another good substitute is Indian curry leaf, which can be found fresh or frozen in Indian markets.

GINGER
Fresh ginger root has a silvery brown skin that must be scraped or peeled. Slice and either chop or pound the flesh, and use quickly for maximum flavor. Bruised ginger is suggested in some recipes: give it a sharp blow with the end of a rolling pin or use a mortar and pestle. Store in the fridge salad tray, wrapped tightly in paper towels.

Chopped ginger is available in jars and keeps well in the fridge.

LEMON GRASS
An essential ingredient in the cooking of South-east Asia, lemon grass has a magical aroma and flavor. Fresh stems are easy to find in supermarkets, Asian stores and good vegetable markets. To prepare for a spice paste, for instance, discard the root end and then cut the lower 2½ inches. Slice the lower, bulbous piece and grind it as directed, then bruise the top half and add it to the curry to infuse its flavor or use it as a brush with which to baste the meat on saté sticks. Wrap closely in paper towels or newspaper and store in the salad tray in the fridge. Fresh, ground lemon grass is available in jars.

LAOS (greater galangal, lengkuas)
A member of the ginger family, which is used more than ginger in Indonesian cooking. The root is creamy colored, with rings on the skin, and may have pink nodules rather like very young ginger.

To prepare, trim off the required amount. Trim off any knobbly bits, then peel carefully as the skin has an unpleasant taste and is tough. Slice to use in a paste and use up as soon as possible after peeling, to preserve the flavor. The flesh is much more woody and fibrous than ginger and has a distinctive, pine-like smell. Wrap in paper towels or newspaper and store in

From left: fresh cilantro root and leaves, lemon grass and lime leaves.

Clockwise from top left: mango cut in half, whole mango, halved lime and whole limes.

the salad tray in the fridge or freeze it. Dried laos powder can be bought; use 1 teaspoon to replace every inch of fresh laos. The fresh has a better flavor.

LIME LEAVES (duan jeruk)
These glossy, dark green leaves come from the kaffir lime tree and are sold as kaffir lime leaves in Asian stores. They have a pleasing smell and can be torn or left whole. Leaves can be frozen and used straight from the freezer.

MACADAMIA NUTS (kemiri, buah keras and candlenuts)
Popular as a cocktail snack and an essential ingredient in Indonesian cooking. Marble-sized nuts which, when ground, act as a thickening agent in many recipes. For convenience, almonds can be used instead, but do try to find macadamia or even Brazil nuts.

NOODLES (mee/mie)
Add dried egg noodles to a large pan of boiling, salted water and cook for 3–5 minutes. Stir to prevent the noodles from settling on the base of the pan. Drain and rinse with cold water, to wash out starch and prevent the noodles from sticking together.

Fresh egg noodles take only 1 minute to cook in salted, fast-boiling water. Drain as above and then use as directed.

Rice noodles (rice sticks) can be

From left: fresh red chilies, pandan leaves, dried red chilies and dried green chilies.

soaked ahead of cooking, either in cold water for some time, or in warm water for just a few minutes. Plunge into fast-boiling, salted water. Allow to return to the boil, then remove from the heat and let stand for 2 minutes only, until just cooked. Test one piece and then drain and rinse well with cold water, if not using immediately.

Bean thread cellophane noodles (*su-un*) are made from mung bean flour and gathered into a coil. Soak in cold water, cut into lengths with scissors and place in boiling water for 1 minute. Drain and use as required.

PANDAN LEAVES (screwpine)
Leaves like gladioli in size and shape, which impart a warm aroma when cooked. Available fresh, in bunches, pandan leaves are used to flavor rice and desserts. Pull the tines of a fork through a leaf to tear it and release the flavor, and tie the leaf in a knot so that it is easy to find and remove.

RICE
We are more discerning these days about the rice we eat. Without doubt Thai fragrant – or Jasmine – rice

Clockwise from top left: dried whole mushrooms, red-skinned peanuts in their shells, purple-skinned shallots, tamarind with part of the pod removed, and whole tamarind pods.

rightly holds its high reputation for quality and fragrance. Many homes have a rice cooker but if not, use the following method for boiled rice.

Boiled rice: wash 1¼ cups of rice in several changes of water, until the water is clear. Place in a pan, with 2¼ cups of water and bring to a boil. Reduce the heat, stir, cover the pan and cook gently for 12–15 minutes. Stir with a chopstick or roasting fork, so as not to break up the grains. Cover and leave for 3–4 minutes before using; or wrap the pan in a heavy towel to keep the rice warm for 1–1½ hours.

SHRIMP PASTE (terasi blachan, balachan)
An essential ingredient, common to the countries of South-east Asia, made from fermented shrimp, with salt, pounded into a paste and sold in small jars or cans, from 2–8 ounces, in Asian markets. Before using wrap a cube in foil and place in a dry frying pan over a gentle heat for 5 minutes, turning from time to time. This takes away the rawness from the shrimp paste and also avoids filling the kitchen with the strong and distinctive smell. If the

shrimp paste is to be fried in the recipe, this stage of cooking can be omitted.

SOY SAUCE
Soy sauce is made from fermented soybeans, wheat grains, salt and water. There are two main varieties: thick, or black, and thin, oddly known as white! In Indonesia, it is called *kecap asin*. *Kecap sedang* is of medium consistency but ordinary soy sauce, or *kecap manis*, is preferred as it is thicker and sweeter.

TAMARIND (asam jawa)
Tamarind is used to add tartness to recipes. A convenient concentrate is sold in a block. Here, 1 teaspoon of tamarind pulp is mixed with warm water. Let soak, then mix to release the pulp from the seeds. Strain and discard the pulp and seeds. Use as directed. Ready-made juice is available.

TURMERIC
Turmeric is a member of the ginger family. When peeled or scraped, a rich golden root is revealed. It gives a superb color to sauces or rice, as well as a good flavor and a warm aroma. Wear rubber gloves to prevent staining.

EQUIPMENT IN THE KITCHEN

WOK

In Indonesia, the wok is called a *wajan*. There are many different qualities of wok on sale and the best advice is to go for the heaviest quality you can find; thin, lightweight woks are always a disappointment, because you are very likely to burn the food, which is invariably cooked at a high temperature. The wok is ideal, not only for stir-frying, but for deep-frying too. If you have a gas cooker, choose one with a metal stand, on which the wok sits firmly and safely during cooking. There are several types of electric woks on sale, frequently with nonstick surfaces, so you must use wooden or plastic tools with these.

One useful cooking tip is to warm the wok gently before adding the oil for cooking. The oil then floods easily over the surface of the warm pan and prevents food from sticking. The amount of oil needed in a wok is considerably less than required in a conventional pan, which is a real plus-point in these health-conscious days.

FOOD PROCESSOR OR PESTLE AND MORTAR

Both feature countless times in this book in the preparation of spice pastes and the blending of ingredients. When time is short a food processor is invaluable; it is the next-best thing to a

Left: Wok with nonstick surface and closely fitting lid and wooden spatula. The wok can double as a steamer, or food can be kept warm on the rack.

helper in the kitchen. The various blade attachments are useful when thin, even slices of onion, cucumber and so on are required. When preparing spice pastes, fibrous ingredients, such as ginger, laos and lemon grass, are best sliced thinly before processing, to obtain a smoother paste. Alternatively, bruise in the mortar with the pestle first. Some oil can be added to the spice paste ingredients, to ease the blending, but remember to reduce the amount for frying the paste accordingly.

A deep granite pestle and mortar, sold in many oriental stores and markets, which is pitted inside, is ideal for finely pounding the wet spices that are such an important part of the preparation of the spice paste. This may seem laborious to us, in our instant world, but to oriental cooks this is a gratifying and pleasurable activity.

A small coffee grinder is useful where small quantities of dry spices are to be pounded, but it is advisable to keep it exclusively for this purpose.

STEAMERS

Bamboo, stacking-type steamers are available in a host of sizes from a wide range of stores. When not in use, they look very attractive on a shelf in the kitchen. Like almost all utensils in the oriental kitchen, they are multi-purpose. Indeed the baskets can be used for serving as well as cooking the foods. Where small items are being cooked, line the baskets with a piece of rinsed cheesecloth. Several baskets can be stacked one on top of the other, with the lid set on top. These are then placed over the wok and the boiling water replenished as required. For cooking large items, such as a whole

fish in a dish, place in the wok over water, cover with a lid and watch the water level while the food is steaming.

BARBECUE

In Indonesia they often use a special barbecue unit for cooking *satés*, which is very lightweight and requires very little charcoal. A gas or electric broiler can be used, of course, but food that has been cooked over charcoal has an extra special flavor. A large fan, made from woven palm fronds, is used to keep the charcoal glowing. Again, this looks very attractive hanging up in the kitchen, when not in use.

RICE COOKER

These are immensely popular in Indonesia and you can see why, when up to three meals a day can be rice-based. The great advantage of the rice cooker is that it is foolproof, producing perfect rice every time, and will happily keep the rice warm for up to five hours. Leftover rice can be reheated the following day and the cooker may also be used for steaming many other dishes.

Above: Attractive two-tiered bamboo steamer with lid, useful for meat or fish and vegetable dishes which are to be steamed together.

SOUPS AND SNACKS

All around the clock, in cities, towns and large villages, warungs – or street vendors – provide nourishing snack food at a moment's notice. The krupuk (shrimp cracker) seller has two huge containers, like large dustbins, suspended at either end of a bamboo pole; he moves along at full speed. Satés are a great favorite; these delicious morsels of beef, shrimp, pork or lamb on bamboo skewers, served with either a peanut or soy-based sauce, need no introduction. Soup is not served as a separate course but used to moisten a bowl of rice, with other dishes and accompaniments ranged around it. Soto is a main-course soup; sop is a clear soup with meat, chicken and some vegetables. Sayur is a vegetable soup, often made with a coconut-flavored stock.

Spicy Meat Patties with Coconut

Spicy meat patties, known as *Rempah*, with a hint of coconut, often feature as one of the delicious accompaniments in an Indonesian-style buffet.

INGREDIENTS

Makes 22
4 ounces freshly grated coconut, or dried coconut, soaked in 4–6 tablespoons boiling water
12 ounces finely ground beef
½ teaspoon each coriander and cumin seeds, dry-fried
1 garlic clove, crushed
a little beaten egg
1–2 tablespoons flour
peanut oil for frying
salt
thin lemon or lime wedges, to serve

1 Mix the moistened coconut with the ground beef.

2 Grind the dry-fried coriander and cumin seeds with a mortar and pestle. Add the ground spices to the meat and coconut mixture together with the garlic, salt to taste, and sufficient beaten egg to bind.

3 Divide the meat into even-size portions, the size of a walnut, and form into patty shapes.

4 Dust with flour. Heat the oil and then fry the patties for 4–5 minutes until both sides are golden brown and cooked through. Serve with lemon or lime wedges, to squeeze over.

Corn Fritters

There is no doubt that freshly cooked corn is best for this recipe, called *Perkedel Jagung*. Do not add salt to the water, because this toughens the outer husk.

INGREDIENTS

Makes 20
2 fresh corn on the cob, or 12-ounce can corn kernels
2 macadamia nuts or 4 almonds
1 garlic clove
1 onion, quartered
½ inch fresh *laos*, peeled and sliced
1 teaspoon ground coriander
2–3 tablespoons oil
3 eggs, beaten
2 tablespoons dried coconut
2 scallions, finely shredded
a few celery leaves, finely shredded (optional)
salt

1 Cook the corn on the cob in boiling water for 7–8 minutes. Drain, cool slightly and, using a sharp knife, strip the kernels from the cob. If using canned corn kernels, drain well.

2 Grind the nuts, garlic, onion, *laos* and coriander to a fine paste in a food processor or mortar and pestle. Heat a little oil and fry the paste until it gives off a spicy aroma.

3 Add the fried spices to the beaten eggs with the coconut, scallions and celery leaves, if using. Add salt to taste with the corn kernels.

4 Heat the remaining oil in a shallow frying pan. Drop large spoonfuls of batter into the pan and cook for about 2–3 minutes until golden. Flip the fritters over with a metal spatula and cook until golden brown and crispy. Cook three or four fritters at a time.

Clear Soup with Meatballs

INGREDIENTS

Serves 8

For the meatballs

6 ounces very finely ground beef
1 small onion, very finely chopped
1–2 garlic cloves, crushed
1 tablespoon cornstarch
a little egg white, lightly beaten
salt and freshly ground black pepper

For the soup

4–6 Chinese mushrooms, soaked in
   warm water for 30 minutes
2 tablespoons peanut oil
1 large onion, finely chopped
2 garlic cloves, finely crushed
½ inch fresh ginger root, bruised
8 cups beef or chicken broth, including
   strained soaking liquid from
   the mushrooms
2 tablespoons soy sauce
4 ounces spinach or Chinese
   cabbage, shredded

1 First prepare the meatballs. Mix the beef with the onion, garlic, cornstarch and seasoning in a food processor and then bind with sufficient egg white to make a firm mixture. With dampened hands, roll into tiny, bite-size balls and set aside.

2 Drain the mushrooms and reserve the soaking liquid to add to the broth. Trim off and discard the stalks. Slice the caps finely and set aside.

3 Heat a large saucepan or wok and add the oil. Fry the onion, garlic and ginger to bring out the flavor, but do not allow to brown.

4 When the onion is soft, pour in the broth. Bring to a boil, then stir in the soy sauce and mushroom slices and simmer for 10 minutes. Add the meatballs and cook for 10 minutes.

5 Just before serving, remove the ginger. Stir in the shredded spinach or Chinese cabbage. Heat through for 1 minute only: no longer or the leaves will be overcooked. Serve the soup immediately.

Tamarind Soup with Peanuts and Vegetables

Sayur Asam is a colorful and refreshing soup from Jakarta with more than a hint of sharpness.

INGREDIENTS

Serves 4 or 8 as part of a buffet
For the spice paste
5 shallots or 1 medium red
  onion, sliced
3 garlic cloves, crushed
1 inch *laos,* peeled and sliced
1–2 fresh red chilies, seeded and sliced
3 tablespoons raw peanuts
1 teaspoon shrimp paste
5 cups well-flavored chicken or
  vegetable broth
½ cup salted peanuts, lightly crushed
1–2 tablespoons dark brown sugar
1 teaspoon tamarind pulp, soaked in
  5 tablespoons warm water for
  15 minutes
salt

For the vegetables
1 chayote, thinly peeled, seeds
  removed, flesh finely sliced
4 ounces green beans, trimmed and
  finely sliced
⅓ cup corn kernels (optional)
handful green leaves, such as
  watercress, arugula or Chinese
  cabbage, finely shredded
1 fresh green chili, sliced, to garnish

1 Prepare the spice paste by grinding the shallots or onion, garlic, *laos,* chilies, raw peanuts and shrimp paste to a paste in a food processor or with a mortar and pestle.

2 Pour in some of the broth to moisten and then pour this mixture into a pan or wok, adding the rest of the broth. Cook for 15 minutes with the lightly crushed peanuts and sugar.

3 Strain the tamarind, discarding the seeds, and reserve the juice.

4 About 5 minutes before serving, add the chayote slices, beans and corn, if using, to the soup and cook fairly rapidly. At the last minute, add the greens or cabbage.

5 Add the tamarind juice and taste for seasoning. Serve, garnished with slices of green chili.

Vegetable Broth with Ground Beef

INGREDIENTS

Serves 6

2 tablespoons peanut oil
4 ounces finely ground beef
1 large onion, grated or finely chopped
1 garlic clove, crushed
1–2 fresh chilies, seeded and chopped
½ teaspoon shrimp paste
3 macadamia nuts or 6 almonds,
    finely ground
1 carrot, finely grated
1 teaspoon brown sugar
4 cups chicken broth
2 ounces dried shrimp, soaked in warm
    water for 10 minutes
8 ounces spinach, cooked, drained and
    finely chopped
8 baby corn, sliced, or 7 ounces canned
    corn kernels
1 large tomato, chopped
juice of ½ lemon
salt

1 Heat the oil in a saucepan. Add the beef, onion and garlic and cook, stirring, until the meat changes color.

2 Add the chilies, shrimp paste, nuts, carrot, sugar and salt to taste.

COOK'S TIP

To make this broth, *Sayur Menir,* very hot and spicy, add the seeds from the chilies.

3 Add the broth and bring gently to a boil. Reduce the heat to a simmer and then add the soaked shrimp, with their soaking liquid. Simmer for about 10 minutes.

4 A few minutes before serving, add the spinach, corn, tomato and lemon juice. Simmer for a minute or two, to heat through. Do not overcook at this stage because this will spoil the appearance and the taste of the *sayur.*

Omelets with Spicy Meat Filling

INGREDIENTS

Serves 4

For the filling

½-inch cube *terasi*
3 garlic cloves, crushed
4 macadamia nuts or 8 almonds
½ inch fresh *laos*, peeled and sliced, or
    1 teaspoon *laos* powder (optional)
1 teaspoon ground coriander
½ teaspoon ground turmeric
1 teaspoon salt
2 tablespoons oil
8 ounces ground beef
2 scallions, chopped
½ celery stalk, finely chopped
2–3 tablespoons coconut milk

For the omelets

oil for frying
4 eggs, beaten with 4 tablespoons
    water
salt and freshly ground black pepper
salad and celery leaves, to serve

1 Grind the *terasi* to a paste, in a food processor or with a mortar and pestle, with the garlic, nuts and fresh *laos*, if using. Add the coriander, turmeric, *laos* powder, (if using), and the salt.

2 Heat the oil and fry the mixture for 1–2 minutes. Stir in the ground beef and cook until it changes color. Cook for 2–3 minutes. Stir in the scallions, celery and coconut milk. Cover and cook gently for 5 minutes.

3 Meanwhile, prepare the omelets. Heat a little oil in an omelet or frying pan. Season the eggs and use to make four thin omelets in the usual way. When each omelet is almost cooked, spoon a quarter of the filling on top and roll up. Keep warm while making the remaining omelets.

4 Cut the rolled omelets in half and arrange on a serving dish. Serve garnished with a few salad and celery leaves.

Spicy Meat-filled Packages

In Indonesia the finest gossamer dough is made for *Martabak*. You can achieve equally good results using ready-made filo pastry or spring roll wrappers.

INGREDIENTS

Makes 16

1 pound lean ground beef
2 small onions, finely chopped
2 small leeks, very
    finely chopped
2 garlic cloves, crushed
2 teaspoons coriander seeds, dry-fried
    and ground
1 teaspoon cumin seeds, dry-fried
    and ground
1–2 teaspoons mild curry powder
2 eggs, beaten
1-pound package filo pastry
3–4 tablespoons sunflower oil
salt and freshly ground black pepper
light soy sauce, to serve

1 To make the filling, mix the meat with the onions, leeks, garlic, coriander, cumin, curry powder and seasoning. Turn into a heated wok, without oil, and stir constantly, until the meat has changed color and looks cooked, about 5 minutes.

2 Allow to cool and then mix in enough beaten egg to bind to a soft consistency. Any leftover egg can be used to seal the edges of the dough; otherwise, use milk.

3 Brush a sheet of filo with oil and lay another sheet on top. Cut the sheets in half. Place a large spoonful of the filling on each double piece of filo. Fold the sides to the middle so that the edges just overlap. Brush these edges with either beaten egg or milk and fold the other two sides to the middle in the same way, so that you now have a square package. Make sure that the package is as flat as possible, to speed cooking. Repeat with the other fifteen packages and place on a floured sheet of wax paper on a tray in the fridge.

4 Heat the remaining oil in a shallow pan and cook several packages at a time, depending on the size of the pan. Cook for 3 minutes on the first side and then turn them over and cook for another 2 minutes, or until heated through. Cook the remaining packages in the same way and serve hot, sprinkled with light soy sauce.

5 If preferred, these spicy packages can be cooked in a hot oven at 400°F for 20 minutes. Glaze with more beaten egg before baking for a rich, golden color.

Pork Satés

Though Indonesia is a Muslim country there have been waves of Chinese immigrants, who have made an enormous contribution to the richness of its cuisine, including the introduction of pork in many recipes. Beef or lamb could be used for *Saté Babi Ketjap* instead.

INGREDIENTS

Makes 12–16 skewers
1¼ pounds pork loin

For the marinade
⅝ cup dark soy sauce
3–4 garlic cloves, crushed
3 tablespoons peanut oil
⅜ cup peanuts, finely
   crushed (optional)
salt and freshly ground black pepper

For the sauce
1 onion, finely chopped
2–3 fresh red chilies, seeded and
   ground, or 1 tablespoon Chili Sambal
⅜ cup dark soy sauce
4–6 tablespoons water
juice of 1–2 limes or 1 large lemon
⅝ cup peanuts, coarsely ground

To serve
lime wedges
Deep-fried Onions

1 Wipe and trim the meat. Cut the pork loin into 1-inch cubes or into thin strips about ½ inch wide by 2 inches long.

2 Blend the dark soy sauce, garlic and oil together with seasoning and the crushed peanuts, if using. Pour over the meat and allow to marinate for at least 1 hour, turning in the marinade from time to time.

3 If using wooden or bamboo skewers, soak them in water for 1 hour so that they don't burn when the *satés* are being cooked. Then thread three or four pieces of meat onto one end of each of the skewers.

4 Make the sauce. Put the onion, chilies or Chili Sambal, soy sauce and water in a saucepan. Bring to a boil, and simmer for 4–5 minutes. Cool, then stir in the lime or lemon juice. Add the coarsely ground peanuts to the sauce just before serving. Preheat the broiler or barbecue grill.

5 Cook the *satés*, turning frequently, until tender, about 5–8 minutes. Garnish with lime wedges and Deep-fried Onions and serve with the sauce.

Peanut Fritters

You can buy rice powder and rice flour in any Asian shop. For this recipe, *Rempeyak Kacang*, it is best to use the rice flour which is ideal as it has a slightly more grainy texture. Peanut fritters are easy and quick to prepare. They go well with Festive Rice and make a good addition to a buffet.

INGREDIENTS

Makes 15–20
½ cup rice flour
½ teaspoon baking powder
1 garlic clove, crushed
½ teaspoon ground coriander
2 pinches ground cumin
½ teaspoon ground turmeric
⅜ cup peanuts, lightly crushed
⅝ cup water, or coconut milk or a
    mixture of both
oil for shallow-frying
salt
cilantro leaves, to garnish

1 Put the rice flour, salt to taste and baking powder in a bowl. Add the garlic, coriander, cumin, turmeric and peanuts. Gradually stir in the water or coconut milk, to make a smooth, slightly runny batter.

2 Heat a little oil in a frying pan. Use a dessertspoon to spoon the batter into the pan and cook several fritters at a time. When the tops are no longer runny and the undersides are lacy and golden brown, turn them over with a spatula and cook the other sides until crisp and brown.

3 Lift out and drain on paper towels. Either use immediately or cool and store in an airtight tin.

4 To reheat the fritters, place in a single layer on a large baking sheet. Bake at 350°F for about 10 minutes. Garnish with cilantro.

COOK'S TIP

You can use either salted or unsalted peanuts in this recipe, but remember to adjust the seasoning accordingly.

Shrimp Crackers

In Indonesia one can find a wide range of *kroepoek* (the "oe" spelling betrays the Dutch influence). They can be made from rice, wheat, corn or cassava and so have differing flavors – rather like our crisps. You may use the tiny Chinese-style shrimp crackers which are more readily available from Asian stores and some large supermarkets.

INGREDIENTS

oil for deep-frying
8-ounce package shrimp crackers, or
    ½ x 1¼-pound package large
    Indonesian shrimp crackers

1 Heat the oil in a deep-frying pan to 375°F, or when a cube of day-old bread browns in 30 seconds.

2 Fry just one of the large *kroepoek* at a time, especially if they are being cooked whole. Cook 8–10 small crackers at a time.

3 As soon as they have expanded and become very puffy, remove them immediately from the oil with a slotted spoon. Do not allow them to color. Drain the crackers on paper towels. They can be cooked a few hours in advance and any leftovers can be kept in an airtight container.

Lamb Satés

INGREDIENTS

Makes 25–30 skewers

2¼-pound leg of lamb, boned
3 garlic cloves, crushed
1–2 tablespoons Chili Sambal or 3–4
   fresh chilies, seeded and ground, or
   1–2 teaspoons chili powder
4–6 tablespoons dark soy sauce
juice of 1 lemon
salt and freshly ground black pepper
oil for brushing

For the sauce

6 garlic cloves, crushed
1 teaspoon Chili Sambal or 2–3 fresh
   chilies, seeded and ground
6 tablespoons dark soy sauce
1½ tablespoons lemon juice
2 tablespoons boiling water

To serve

small onion pieces
cucumber wedges
Compressed Rice Shapes (optional)

1 Cut the lamb into thick slices and then into neat ½-inch cubes. Remove any pieces of gristle but do not trim off any of the fat because this keeps the *satés* moist during cooking and enhances the flavor.

— VARIATION —

Lamb neck fillet is now widely available in supermarkets and can be used instead of boned leg. Brush the lamb fillet with oil before grilling.

2 Blend the garlic, Chili Sambal, ground fresh chilies or chili powder, soy sauce, lemon juice and seasoning to a paste in a food processor or with a mortar and pestle. Pour over the lamb. Cover and set aside in a cool place for at least an hour. Soak wooden or bamboo skewers in water so that they won't burn during cooking.

3 Prepare the sauce. Put the garlic cloves into a bowl. Add the Chili Sambal or chilies, soy sauce, lemon juice and boiling water. Stir well.

4 Thread the meat onto the skewers. Brush with oil and cook under a broiler, turning often. Brush each *saté* with a little of the sauce and serve hot, with small pieces of onion, cucumber and the rice shapes, if using. Serve with the remaining sauce.

Shrimp Satés

For *Saté Udang*, jumbo shrimp look spectacular and taste wonderful. The spicy coconut marinade marries beautifully with the shrimp and is also excellent when used with firm cubes of monkfish or halibut and cooked in the same way.

INGREDIENTS

Makes 4 skewers
12 uncooked jumbo shrimp

For the marinade
¼ teaspoon shrimp paste
1 garlic clove, crushed
1 lemon grass stem, lower 2½ inches sliced, top reserved
3–4 macadamia nuts or 6–8 almonds
½ teaspoon chili powder
salt
oil for frying
8 tablespoons coconut milk
½ teaspoon tamarind pulp, soaked in 2 tablespoons water, then strained and juice reserved

To serve
Peanut Sauce
Compressed Rice Shapes (optional)
cucumber cubes (optional)
lemon wedges

1 Remove the heads from the shrimp. Peel the shrimp and remove the black cord, if liked. Using a small sharp knife, make an incision along the underbody of each shrimp, without cutting it completely in half and open it up like a book. Thread 3 of the shrimp onto each skewer.

2 Make the marinade. Grind the shrimp paste, garlic, lemon grass slices, nuts, chili powder and a little salt to a paste in a food processor or with a mortar and pestle.

3 Fry the paste in oil for 1 minute. Add the coconut milk and tamarind juice. Simmer for 1 minute. Cool. Pour over the shrimp and leave for 1 hour.

4 Cook the shrimp under a hot broiler or on the barbecue grill for 3 minutes or until cooked through. Beat the top part of the lemon grass with the end of a rolling pin, to make it into a brush. Use this to brush the shrimp with the marinade during cooking.

5 Serve on a platter, with the Peanut Sauce, rice shapes and cucumber cubes, if using, and lemon wedges.

Spiced Vegetable Soup with Chicken and Shrimp

INGREDIENTS

Serves 6–8

1 onion, ½ cut in two, ½ sliced
2 garlic cloves, crushed
1 fresh red or green chili, seeded
   and sliced
½ teaspoon shrimp paste
3 macadamia nuts or 6 almonds
½ inch *laos*, peeled and sliced, or 1
   teaspoon *laos* powder
1 teaspoon sugar
oil for frying
8 ounces boned, skinned chicken
   breast, cut in ½-inch cubes
1¼ cups coconut milk
5 cups chicken broth
1 eggplant, diced
8 ounces green beans, chopped
small wedge of crisp white
   cabbage, shredded
1 red bell pepper, seeded and sliced
4 ounces cooked, peeled shrimp
salt and freshly ground black pepper

1 Grind the onion quarters, garlic, chili, shrimp paste, nuts, *laos* and sugar to a paste in a food processor or with a mortar and pestle.

2 Heat a wok, add the oil and then fry the paste, without browning, until it gives off a rich aroma. Add the sliced onion and chicken cubes and cook for 3–4 minutes. Stir in the coconut milk and broth. Bring to a boil and simmer for a few minutes.

3 Add the diced eggplant to the soup, with the beans, and cook for only a few minutes, until the beans are almost cooked.

4 A few minutes before serving, stir the cabbage, bell pepper and shrimp into the soup. The vegetables should be cooked so that they are still crunchy and the shrimp merely heated through. Taste the soup and adjust the seasoning if necessary.

Spiced Beef Satés

INGREDIENTS

Makes 18 skewers

1 pound rump steak, cut in ½-inch
   slices or strips
1 teaspoon coriander seeds, dry-fried
   and ground
½ teaspoon cumin seeds, dry-fried
   and ground
1 teaspoon tamarind pulp
1 small onion
2 garlic cloves
1 tablespoon brown sugar
1 tablespoon dark soy sauce
salt

To serve
cucumber chunks
lemon or lime wedges
Sambal Kecap

1 Mix the meat and spices in a non-metallic bowl. Soak the tamarind pulp in ⅓ cup water.

2 Strain the tamarind and reserve the juice. Put the onion, garlic, tamarind juice, sugar and soy sauce in a food processor and blend well. Alternatively, pound the onion and garlic in a mortar with a pestle, and add the remaining ingredients.

3 Pour the marinade over the meat and spices in the bowl and toss well together. Set aside for at least 1 hour. Meanwhile, soak some bamboo skewers in water to prevent them from burning while cooking.

4 Preheat the broiler. Thread 5 or 6 pieces of meat onto each of the skewers and sprinkle the meat with salt. Place under the hot broiler, or even better, over a charcoal barbecue, and cook, turning frequently, until tender. Baste with the marinade throughout the cooking, turning the skewers over from time to time.

5 Serve on a platter garnished with cucumber chunks and wedges of lemon or lime to squeeze over the *satés*. Put the *Sambal Kecap* in a small bowl and serve alongside.

Deep-fried Wonton Pillows with Sambal Kecap

Pangsit Goreng are popular as party fare or for a quick snack.

INGREDIENTS

Makes 40

4 ounces pork loin, trimmed
  and sliced
8 ounces cooked, peeled shrimp
2–3 garlic cloves, crushed
2 scallions, coarsely chopped
1 tablespoon cornstarch
about 40 wonton wrappers
oil for deep-frying
salt and freshly ground black pepper

For the Sambal Kecap

1–2 fresh red chilies, seeded and sliced
1–2 garlic cloves, crushed
3 tablespoons dark soy sauce
3–4 tablespoons lemon or lime juice
1–2 tablespoons water

1 Grind the slices of pork finely in a food processor. Add the shrimp, garlic, scallions and cornstarch. Season to taste and then process briefly.

2 Place a little of the prepared filling onto each wonton wrapper, just off center, with the wrapper shaped like a diamond in front of you. Dampen all the edges, except for the uppermost corner of the diamond.

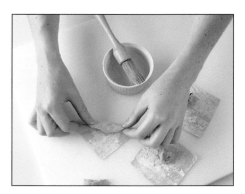

3 Lift the corner nearest to you towards the filling and then roll up the wrapper once more, to cover the filling. Turn over. Bring the two extreme corners together, sealing one on top of the other. Squeeze lightly, to plump up the filling. Repeat until all the wrappers and the filling are used up. The prepared "pillows" can be frozen at this stage. Any leftover wonton wrappers can be wrapped and stored in the freezer as well.

4 Meanwhile, prepare the Sambal. Mix the chilies and garlic together and then stir in the dark soy sauce, lemon or lime juice and water. Pour into a serving bowl and set aside.

5 Heat the oil in a deep-frying pan to 375°F, or when a cube of day-old bread browns in 30 seconds. Deep-fry the wonton pillows, a few at a time, for about 2–3 minutes, or until cooked through, crisp and golden brown. Remove with a slotted spoon and drain on paper towels. If cooking from frozen, allow 4 minutes. Serve on a large platter together with the Sambal Kecap.

Balinese Vegetable Soup

Any seasonal vegetables can be used in *Sayur Oelih*.

INGREDIENTS

Serves 8

8 ounces green beans
5 cups boiling water
1²/₃ cups coconut milk
1 garlic clove
2 macadamia nuts or 4 almonds
½ teaspoon shrimp paste
2–3 teaspoons coriander seeds, dry-
    fried and ground
oil for frying
1 onion, finely sliced
2 *duan salam* or bay leaves
8 ounces bean sprouts
2 tablespoons lemon juice
salt

1 Remove the ends from the green beans and cut into small pieces. Cook the beans in the salted, boiling water for 3–4 minutes. Drain the beans and reserve the cooking water.

2 Spoon off 3–4 tablespoons of the cream from the top of the coconut milk and reserve it.

3 Grind the garlic, nuts, shrimp paste, and ground coriander together to a paste in a food processor or with a mortar and pestle.

4 Heat the oil in a wok or saucepan, and fry the onion until transparent. Remove and reserve. Fry the paste for 2 minutes without browning. Pour in the reserved vegetable water and coconut milk. Bring to a boil and add the *duan salam* or bay leaves. Cook, uncovered, for 15–20 minutes.

5 Just before serving, add the beans, fried onion, bean sprouts, reserved coconut cream and lemon juice. Taste for seasoning and adjust it, if necessary. Serve at once.

COOK'S TIP

Even in the East, cooks use canned coconut milk. Any leftovers can be chilled for 3–4 days or frozen immediately, then thawed before use.

FISH AND SEAFOOD

There is a seemingly endless variety of fish available in Indonesian markets. In Jakarta's fish market oil-skinned and rubber-booted young men carry enormous baskets of fish on bamboo poles to the auction area. Mackerel, tuna, mullet, ikan merah (snapper) and cumi (squid) all feature, as well as superb shellfish, crabs and huge shrimp.

These recipes illustrate the delicious variety of Indonesian fish cuisine. Serving quantities assume you will be eating them as main courses, perhaps with rice and a salad or vegetable accompaniment. They will serve more people as part of a buffet.

Spicy Fish

If you make *Ikan Kecap* a day ahead, put it straight onto a serving dish after cooking and then pour over the sauce, cover and chill until required.

INGREDIENTS

Serves 3–4
1 pound fish fillets, such as mackerel, cod or haddock
2 tablespoons flour
peanut oil for frying
1 onion, coarsely chopped
1 small garlic clove, crushed
1½ inches fresh ginger root, peeled and grated
1–2 fresh red chilies, seeded and sliced
½ teaspoon shrimp paste
4 tablespoons water
juice of ½ lemon
1 tablespoon brown sugar
2 tablespoons dark soy sauce
salt
roughly torn lettuce leaves, to serve

1 Rinse the fish fillets under cold water and dry well on absorbent paper towels. Cut into serving portions and remove any bones.

2 Season the flour with salt and use it to dust the fish. Heat the oil in a frying pan and fry the fish on both sides for 3–4 minutes, or until cooked. Lift onto a plate and set aside.

3 Rinse out and dry the pan. Heat a little more oil and fry the onion, garlic, ginger and chilies just to bring out the flavor. Do not brown.

4 Blend the shrimp paste with a little water, to make a paste. Add it to the onion mixture, with a little extra water if necessary. Cook for 2 minutes and then stir in the lemon juice, brown sugar and soy sauce.

5 Pour over the fish and serve, hot or cold, with roughly torn lettuce.

COOK'S TIP

For a buffet dish cut the fish into bite-size pieces or serving portions.

Squid from Madura

This squid dish, *Cumi Cumi Madura*, is popular in Indonesia. It is quite usual to be invited into the restaurant kitchen and given a warm welcome.

INGREDIENTS

Serves 2–3
1 pound cleaned and drained squid, body cut in strips, tentacles left whole
3 garlic cloves
¼ teaspoon ground nutmeg
1 bunch of scallions
4 tablespoons sunflower oil
1 cup water
1 tablespoon dark soy sauce
salt and freshly ground black pepper
1 lime, cut in wedges (optional)
boiled rice, to serve

1 Squeeze out and discard the little central "bone" from each tentacle. Heat a wok, toss in the squid and stir-fry for 1 minute. Remove the squid.

2 Crush the garlic with the nutmeg and some salt and pepper. Trim the roots from the scallions, cut the white part into small pieces, slice the green part and then set aside.

3 Heat the wok, add the oil and fry the white part of the scallions. Stir in the garlic paste and the squid.

4 Rinse out the garlic paste container with the water and soy sauce and add to the pan. Half-cover and simmer for 4–5 minutes. Add the scallion tops, toss lightly and serve at once, with lime, if using, and rice.

Whole Fish with Sweet and Sour Sauce

INGREDIENTS

Serves 4

1 whole fish, such as red snapper or
  carp, about 2¼ pounds prepared
2–3 tablespoons cornstarch
oil for frying
salt and freshly ground black pepper
boiled rice, to serve

For the spice paste

2 garlic cloves
2 lemon grass stems
1 inch fresh *laos*
1 inch fresh ginger root
¾ inch fresh turmeric or
  ½ teaspoon ground turmeric
5 macadamia nuts or 10 almonds

For the sauce

1 tablespoon brown sugar
3 tablespoons cider vinegar
about 1½ cups water
2 lime leaves, torn
4 shallots, quartered
3 tomatoes, skinned and cut in wedges
3 scallions, finely shredded
1 fresh red chili, seeded and shredded

1 Wash and dry the fish thoroughly and then sprinkle it inside and out with salt. Set aside for 15 minutes, while preparing the other ingredients.

2 Peel and crush the garlic cloves. Use only the lower white part of the lemon grass stems and slice thinly. Peel and slice the fresh *laos*, the ginger root and turmeric, if using. Grind the nuts, garlic, lemon grass, *laos*, ginger and turmeric to a fine paste in a food processor or with a mortar and pestle.

3 Scrape the paste into a bowl. Stir in the brown sugar, cider vinegar, seasoning to taste and the water. Add the lime leaves.

4 Dust the fish with the cornstarch and fry on both sides in hot oil for about 8–9 minutes or until almost cooked through. Drain the fish on paper towels and transfer to a serving dish. Keep warm.

5 Pour off most of the oil and then pour in the spicy liquid and allow to come to a boil. Reduce the heat and cook for 3–4 minutes. Add the shallots and tomatoes, followed a minute later by the scallions and chili. Taste and adjust the seasoning.

6 Pour the sauce over the fish. Serve at once, with plenty of rice.

Spicy Squid

This aromatically spiced squid dish, *Cumi Cumi Smoor*, is a favorite in Madura, and is simple yet delicious. Gone are the days when cleaning squid was such a chore: now they can be bought already cleaned and are available from fish stores, market stalls or from the freezer or fish counters of large supermarkets.

INGREDIENTS

Serves 3–4

1½ pounds squid, rinsed and drained
3 tablespoons peanut oil
1 onion, finely chopped
2 garlic cloves, crushed
1 beefsteak tomato, skinned
  and chopped
1 tablespoon dark soy sauce
½ teaspoon ground nutmeg
6 whole cloves
juice of ½ lemon or lime
salt and freshly ground black pepper
boiled rice, to serve

1 Cut squid into ribbons and remove the "bone" from each tentacle.

2 Heat a wok, toss in the squid and stir constantly for 2–3 minutes, when the squid will have curled into attractive shapes or into firm rings. Lift out and set aside in a warm place.

3 Heat the oil in a clean pan and fry the onion and garlic, until soft and beginning to brown. Add the tomato, soy sauce, nutmeg, cloves, ⅔ cup water and lemon or lime juice. Bring to a boil, reduce the heat and add the squid with seasoning to taste.

4 Cook gently for 3–5 minutes more, uncovered, stirring from time to time. Take care not to overcook the squid. Serve hot or warm, with boiled rice, or as part of a buffet spread.

— VARIATION —

Instead of squid try using 1 pound cooked and peeled large shrimp in this recipe. Add them for the final 1–2 minutes.

Shrimp with Chayote in Turmeric Sauce

This delicious, attractively colored dish is called *Gule Udang Dengan Labu Kuning*.

INGREDIENTS

Serves 4

1–2 chayotes or 2–3 zucchini
2 fresh red chilies, seeded
1 onion, quartered
¼ inch fresh *laos*, peeled
1 lemon grass stem, lower 2 inches sliced, top bruised
1 inch fresh turmeric, peeled
⅞ cup water
lemon juice
14-ounce can coconut milk
1 pound cooked, peeled shrimp
salt
red chili shreds, to garnish (optional)
boiled rice, to serve

1 Peel the chayotes, remove the seeds and cut into strips. If using zucchini, cut into 2-inch strips.

2 Grind the fresh red chilies, onion, sliced *laos*, sliced lemon grass and the fresh turmeric to a paste in a food processor or with a mortar and pestle. Add the water to the paste mixture, with a squeeze of lemon juice and salt to taste.

3 Pour into a pan. Add the top of the lemon grass stem. Bring to the boil and cook for 1–2 minutes. Add the chayote or zucchini pieces and cook for 2 minutes. Stir in the coconut milk. Taste and adjust the seasoning.

4 Stir in the shrimp and cook gently for 2–3 minutes. Remove the lemon grass stem. Garnish with shreds of chili, if using, and serve with rice.

Doedoeh of Fish

Haddock or cod fillet may be substituted in this recipe.

INGREDIENTS

Serves 6–8

2¼ pounds fresh mackerel fillets, skinned
2 tablespoons tamarind pulp, soaked in ⅞ cup water
1 onion
½ inch fresh *laos*
2 garlic cloves
1–2 fresh red chilies, seeded, or 1 teaspoon chili powder
1 teaspoon ground coriander
1 teaspoon ground turmeric
½ teaspoon ground fennel seeds
1 tablespoon dark brown sugar
6–7 tablespoons oil
⅞ cup coconut cream
salt and freshly ground black pepper
fresh chili shreds, to garnish

1 Rinse the fish fillets in cold water and dry them well on paper towels. Put into a shallow dish and sprinkle with a little salt. Strain the tamarind and pour the juice over the fish fillets. Set aside for 30 minutes.

2 Quarter the onion, peel and slice the *laos* and peel the garlic. Grind the onion, *laos*, garlic and chilies or chili powder to a paste in a food processor or with a mortar and pestle. Add the ground coriander, turmeric, fennel seeds and sugar.

3 Heat half of the oil in a frying pan. Drain the fish fillets and fry for 5 minutes, or until cooked. Set aside.

4 Wipe out the pan and heat the remaining oil. Fry the spice paste, stirring constantly, until it gives off a spicy aroma. Do not let it brown. Add the coconut cream and simmer gently for a few minutes. Add the fish fillets and gently heat through.

5 Taste for seasoning and serve sprinkled with shredded chili.

Chili Crabs

It is possible to find variations on *Kepitang Pedas* all over Asia. It will be memorable whether you eat it in simple surroundings or in an elegant restaurant.

INGREDIENTS

Serves 4
2 cooked crabs, about 1½ pounds
½ teaspoon shrimp paste
2 garlic cloves
2 fresh red chilies, seeded, or
  1 teaspoon chopped chili from a jar
½ inch fresh ginger root, peeled
  and sliced
4 tablespoons sunflower oil
1¼ cups tomato ketchup
1 tablespoon dark brown sugar
½ cup warm water
4 scallions, chopped, to garnish
cucumber chunks and hot toast,
  to serve (optional)

1 Remove the large claws of one crab and turn onto its back with the head facing away from you. Use your thumbs to push the body up from the main shell. Discard the stomach sac and "dead men's fingers," i.e. lungs and any green matter. Leave the creamy brown meat in the shell and cut the shell in half with a cleaver or heavy knife. Cut the body section in half and crack the claws with a sharp blow from a hammer or cleaver. Avoid splintering the claws. Repeat with the other crab.

2 Grind the shrimp paste, garlic, chilies and ginger in a food processor or with a mortar and pestle.

3 Heat a wok and add the oil. Fry the spice paste, stirring it constantly, without browning.

4 Stir in the tomato ketchup, sugar and water and mix the sauce well. When just boiling, add all the crab pieces and toss in the sauce until well-coated and hot. Serve in a large bowl, sprinkled with the spring onions. Place in the center of the table for everyone to help themselves. Accompany this finger-licking dish with cool cucumber chunks and hot toast for mopping up the sauce, if you like.

Boemboe Bali of Fish

The island of Bali has wonderful fish, surrounded as it is by the sparkling blue sea. This simple fish "curry" is packed with many of the characteristic flavors associated with Indonesia.

INGREDIENTS

Serves 4–6

1½ pounds cod or haddock fillet
½ teaspoon shrimp paste
2 red or white onions
1 inch fresh ginger root, peeled
  and sliced
½ inch fresh *laos*, peeled and sliced, or
  1 teaspoon *laos* powder
2 garlic cloves
1–2 fresh red chilies, seeded, or
  2 teaspoons Chili Sambal, or
  1–2 teaspoons chili powder
6–8 tablespoons sunflower oil
1 tablespoon dark soy sauce
1 teaspoon tamarind pulp, soaked in
  2 tablespoons warm water
1 cup water
celery leaves or chopped fresh chili,
  to garnish
boiled rice, to serve

1 Skin the fish, remove any bones and then cut the flesh into bite-size pieces. Pat dry with paper towels and set aside.

2 Grind the shrimp paste, onions, ginger, *laos*, garlic and fresh chilies, if using, to a paste in a food processor or with a mortar and pestle. Stir in the Chili Sambal or chili powder and *laos* powder, if using.

3 Heat 2 tablespoons of the oil and fry the spice mixture, stirring, until it gives off a rich aroma. Add the soy sauce. Strain the tamarind and add the juice and water. Cook for 2–3 minutes.

--- VARIATION ---

Substitute 1 pound cooked large shrimp. Add them 3 minutes before the end.

4 In a separate pan, fry the fish in the remaining oil for 2–3 minutes. Turn only once so that the pieces stay whole. Lift out with a slotted spoon and put into the sauce.

5 Cook the fish in the sauce for 3 minutes more and serve with boiled rice. Garnish the dish with feathery celery leaves or a little chopped fresh chili, if liked.

Baked or Grilled Spiced Whole Fish

INGREDIENTS

Serves 6

2¼ pounds red snapper or striped bass,
   cleaned and scaled if necessary
1 fresh red chili, seeded and ground, or
   1 teaspoon minced chili from a jar
4 garlic cloves, crushed
1 inch fresh ginger root, sliced
4 scallions, chopped
juice of ½ lemon
2 tablespoons sunflower oil
salt
boiled rice, to serve

1 Rinse the fish and dry it well inside and out with paper towels. Using a sharp knife, slash two or three times through the fleshy part on each side of the fish.

2 Place the chili, garlic, ginger and spring onions in a food processor and blend to a paste, or grind the mixture together with a mortar and pestle. Add the lemon juice and salt, then stir in the oil.

3 Spoon a little of the mixture inside the fish and pour the rest over the top. Turn the fish to coat it completely in the spice mixture and leave to marinate for at least an hour.

4 Preheat the broiler. Place a long strip of double foil under the fish to support it and to make turning it over easier. Put on a rack in the broiler and cook for 5 minutes on one side and 8 minutes on the second side, basting with the marinade during cooking. Serve with boiled rice.

Vinegar Fish

INGREDIENTS

Serves 2–3

2–3 medium-size mackerel, filleted
2–3 fresh red chilies, seeded
4 macadamia nuts or 8 almonds
1 red onion, quartered
2 garlic cloves, crushed
½ inch fresh ginger root, peeled
   and sliced
1 teaspoon ground turmeric
3 tablespoons coconut or vegetable oil
3 tablespoons wine vinegar
⅝ cup water
salt
Deep-fried Onions, to garnish
finely chopped fresh chili, to garnish

1 Rinse the fish fillets in cold water and then dry them well on paper towels. Set aside.

2 Grind the chilies, nuts, onion, garlic, ginger, turmeric and 1 tablespoon of the oil to a paste in a food processor or with a mortar and pestle. Heat the remaining oil in a frying pan and cook the paste for 1–2 minutes without browning. Stir in the vinegar and water. Add salt to taste. Bring to a boil, then simmer.

3 Place the fish fillets in the sauce. Cover and cook for 6–8 minutes, or until the fish is tender.

4 Lift the fish onto a plate and keep warm. Reduce the sauce by boiling rapidly for 1 minute. Pour over the fish and serve. Garnish with Deep-fried Onions and chopped chili.

MEAT
AND
POULTRY

Meat is expensive in Indonesia, so with more than a touch of skill and ingenuity a little is made to go a long way, by adding vegetables, rice and so on. Chicken is very popular. In many recipes chicken is marinated or cooked in a variety of "wet" spices, laos, lemon grass, turmeric and frequently coconut milk, which transform the humble bird into something special. Ducks are also commonly used and steamed Balinese Spiced Duck is especially characteristic. The substantial Chinese population has contributed some delicious duck recipes and it is also responsible for the few dishes that use pork, which is not widely eaten in this primarily Islamic country. Rendang is one of the most popular and well-known Indonesian dishes.

Rendang

INGREDIENTS

Serves 6–8

2¼ pounds prime beef in one piece
2 onions or 5–6 shallots, sliced
4 garlic cloves, crushed
1 inch fresh *laos*, peeled and sliced, or
  1 teaspoon *laos* powder
1 inch fresh ginger root, peeled
  and sliced
4–6 fresh red chilies, seeded and sliced
1 lemon grass stem, lower part, sliced
1 inch fresh turmeric, peeled and
  sliced, or 1 teaspoon ground turmeric
1 teaspoon coriander seeds, dry-fried
  and ground
1 teaspoon cumin seeds, dry-fried
  and ground
2 lime leaves
1 teaspoon tamarind pulp, soaked in
  4 tablespoons warm water
2 x 14-fluid ounce cans coconut milk
1¼ cups water
2 tablespoons dark soy sauce
8 small new potatoes, scrubbed
salt
Deep-fried Onions, to garnish

1 Cut the meat in long strips and then into pieces of even size and place in a bowl.

2 Grind the onions or shallots, garlic, *laos* or *laos* powder, ginger, chilies, sliced lemon grass and turmeric to a fine paste in a food processor or with a mortar and pestle.

3 Add the paste to the meat with the coriander and cumin and mix well. Tear the lime leaves and add them to the mixture. Cover and leave in a cool place to marinate while you prepare the other ingredients.

4 Strain the tamarind and reserve the juice. Pour the coconut milk, water and the tamarind juice into a wok or flameproof casserole and stir in the spiced meat and soy sauce. Add seasoning as desired.

5 Stir until the liquid comes to a boil and then reduce the heat and simmer gently, half-covered, for about 1½–2 hours or until the meat is tender and the liquid reduced.

6 Add the new potatoes about 20–25 minutes before the end of the cooking time. The potatoes will absorb some of the sauce, so add a little more water to compensate if you prefer the Rendang to be rather more moist than it is in Indonesia.

7 Adjust the seasoning and transfer to a serving bowl. Serve garnished with the crisp Deep-fried Onions.

COOK'S TIP

This is even better cooked a day or two in advance, to allow the flavors to mellow. Stop at the end of step 5 and add the potatoes when you reheat.

Grilled Chicken

The flavor of this dish, known in Indonesia as *Ayam Bakur*, will be more intense if the chicken is marinated overnight. It is an ideal recipe for a party, because the final broiling, barbecuing or baking can be done at the last minute. Rock Cornish hens look even more attractive, but remember that they will need less cooking time than chicken quarters, for instance. Sweet and Sour Fruit and Vegetable Salad makes a perfect accompaniment for this broiled chicken dish.

INGREDIENTS

Serves 4

3–3½-pound chicken or 2 Rock
    Cornish hens
4 garlic cloves, crushed
2 lemon grass stems, lower
    2 inches sliced
½ inch fresh *laos*, peeled and sliced
1 teaspoon ground turmeric
2 cups water
3–4 bay leaves
3 tablespoons each dark and light
    soy sauce
¼ cup butter or margarine
salt
boiled rice, to serve

2 Grind the garlic, sliced lemon grass, *laos*, turmeric and salt together into a paste in a food processor or with a mortar and pestle. Rub the paste into the chicken pieces and leave for at least 30 minutes. Wear rubber gloves for this, as the turmeric will stain heavily; or wash your hands immediately after mixing, if you prefer.

4 Just before serving, add the two soy sauces to the pan together with the butter or margarine.

5 Cook until the chicken or hens are well-coated and the sauce has almost been absorbed. Transfer the chicken or hen pieces to a preheated broiler or barbecue, or an oven preheated to 400°F, to complete the cooking. Cook for 10–15 minutes more, turning the pieces often so they become golden brown all over. Take care not to let them burn. Baste with remaining sauce during cooking. Serve with boiled rice.

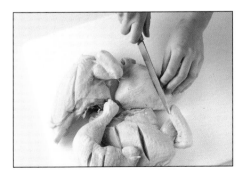

1 Cut the chicken into four or eight portions. Halve the hens or quarter them, if you are serving this as part of a buffet. Slash the fleshy part of each portion twice and set aside.

3 Transfer the chicken or hen pieces to a wok and pour in the water. Add the bay leaves and bring to a boil. Cover and cook gently for 30 minutes, adding a little more water if necessary. Stir from time to time.

Chicken with Turmeric

INGREDIENTS

Serves 4

3–3½-pound chicken, cut in 8 pieces,
    or 4 chicken quarters, each halved
1 tablespoon sugar
3 macadamia nuts or 6 almonds
2 garlic cloves, crushed
1 large onion, quartered
1 inch fresh *laos*, peeled and sliced, or
    1 teaspoon *laos* powder
1–2 lemon grass stems, lower 2 inches
    sliced, top bruised
½ teaspoon shrimp paste
1½ inches fresh turmeric, peeled and
    sliced, or 1 tablespoon
    ground turmeric
1 tablespoon tamarind pulp, soaked in
    ⅔ cup warm water
4–6 tablespoons oil
1⅔ cup coconut milk
salt and freshly ground black pepper
Deep-fried Onions, to garnish

1 Rub the chicken joints with a little sugar and set them aside.

2 Grind the nuts and garlic in a food processor with the onion, *laos*, sliced lemon grass, shrimp paste, and turmeric. Alternatively, pound the ingredients to a paste with a mortar and pestle. Strain the tamarind pulp and reserve the juice.

3 Heat the oil in a wok and cook the paste, without browning, until it gives off a spicy aroma. Add the pieces of chicken and toss well in the spices. Add the strained tamarind juice. Spoon the coconut cream off the top of the milk and set it to one side.

4 Add the coconut milk to the pan. Cover and cook for 45 minutes, or until the chicken is tender.

5 Just before serving, stir in the coconut cream while bringing to a boil. Season and serve at once, garnished with Deep-fried Onions.

Chicken Cooked in Coconut Milk

Traditionally, the chicken pieces would be part-cooked by frying, but roasting in the oven is a better option. *Ayam Opor* is an unusual recipe in that the sauce is white as it does not contain chilies or turmeric, unlike many other Indonesian dishes. The dish is usually served with crisp Deep-fried Onions.

INGREDIENTS

Serves 4

3–3½-pound chicken or
    4 chicken quarters
4 garlic cloves
1 onion, sliced
4 macadamia nuts or 8 almonds
1 tablespoon coriander seeds, dry-fried,
    or 1 teaspoon ground coriander
3 tablespoons oil
1 inch fresh *laos*, peeled
    and bruised
2 lemon grass stems, fleshy part bruised
3 lime leaves
2 bay leaves
1 teaspoon sugar
2½ cups coconut milk
salt
boiled rice and Deep-fried Onions,
    to serve

1 Preheat the oven to 375°F. Cut the chicken into four or eight pieces. Season with salt. Put in an oiled roasting pan and cook in the oven for 25–30 minutes. Meanwhile, prepare the sauce.

2 Grind the garlic, onion, nuts and coriander to a fine paste in a food processor or with a mortar and pestle. Heat the oil and fry the paste to bring out the flavor. Do not allow it to brown.

3 Add the part-cooked chicken pieces to a wok together with the *laos*, lemon grass, lime and bay leaves, sugar, coconut milk and salt to taste. Mix well to coat in the sauce.

4 Bring to a boil and then reduce the heat and simmer gently for 30–40 minutes, uncovered, until the chicken is tender and the coconut sauce is reduced and thickened. Stir the mixture occasionally during cooking.

5 Just before serving remove the bruised *laos* and lemon grass. Serve with boiled rice and sprinkle with Deep-fried Onions.

Aromatic Chicken from Madura

Magadip is best cooked ahead so that the flavors permeate the chicken flesh making it even more delicious. A cool cucumber salad is a good accompaniment.

INGREDIENTS

Serves 4

3–3½-pound chicken, cut in quarters, or 4 chicken quarters
1 teaspoon sugar
2 tablespoons coriander seeds
2 teaspoons cumin seeds
6 whole cloves
½ teaspoon ground nutmeg
½ teaspoon ground turmeric
1 small onion
1 inch fresh ginger root, peeled and sliced
1¼ cups chicken broth or water
salt and freshly ground black pepper
boiled rice and Deep-fried Onions, to serve

1 Cut each chicken quarter in half to obtain eight pieces. Place in a flameproof casserole, sprinkle with sugar and salt and toss together. This helps release the juices in the chicken. Use the backbone and any remaining carcass to make chicken stock for use later in the recipe, if you like.

2 Dry-fry the coriander, cumin and whole cloves until the spices give off a good aroma. Add the nutmeg and turmeric and heat briefly. Grind in a processor or with a mortar and pestle.

— COOK'S TIP —

Add a large piece of bruised ginger and a small onion to the chicken stock to ensure a good flavor.

3 If using a processor, put in the onion and ginger until finely chopped. Otherwise, finely chop the onion and ginger and pound to a paste with a mortar and pestle. Add the spices and broth or water and mix well.

4 Pour over the chicken in the flameproof casserole. Cover with a lid and cook over a gentle heat until the chicken pieces are really tender, about 45–50 minutes.

5 Serve portions of the chicken, with the sauce, on boiled rice, sprinkled with crisp Deep-fried Onions.

Chicken with Spices and Soy Sauce

A very simple recipe, called *Ayam Kecap,* which will often appear as one of the dishes on a Padang restaurant menu. Any leftovers taste equally good when reheated the following day.

INGREDIENTS

Serves 4

3–3½-pound chicken, jointed and cut
  in 16 pieces
3 onions, sliced
about 4 cups water
3 garlic cloves, crushed
3–4 fresh red chilies, seeded and sliced,
  or 1 tablespoon chili powder
3–4 tablespoons oil
½ teaspoon ground nutmeg
6 whole cloves
1 teaspoon tamarind pulp, soaked in
  3 tablespoons warm water
2–3 tablespoons dark or light
  soy sauce
salt
fresh red chili shreds, to garnish
boiled rice, to serve

1 Prepare the chicken and place the pieces in a large pan with one of the onions. Pour over enough water to just cover. Bring to a boil and then reduce the heat and simmer gently for 20 minutes.

2 Grind the remaining onions, with the garlic and chilies, to a fine paste in a food processor or with a mortar and pestle. Heat a little of the oil in a wok or frying pan and cook the paste to bring out the flavor, but do not allow to brown.

3 When the chicken has cooked for about 20 minutes, lift it out of the stock in the pan with a slotted spoon. Transfer the chicken to the pan with the spicy paste mixture. Toss all together over a fairly high heat so that the spices can permeate the chicken pieces. Reserve 1¼ cups of the chicken stock to add to the pan later.

4 Stir in the nutmeg and cloves. Strain the tamarind and add the tamarind juice and the soy sauce to the chicken. Cook for 2–3 minutes more, then add the reserved stock.

5 Taste and adjust the seasoning and cook, uncovered, for another 25–35 minutes, until the chicken pieces are tender.

6 Serve the chicken in a bowl, topped with shredded chili, and eat with boiled rice.

COOK'S TIP

Dark soy sauce is thicker and more salty than light. Adding the dark variety will give a deeper color to the chicken.

Spicy Meat Fritters

INGREDIENTS

Makes 30

1 pound potatoes, boiled and drained
1 pound lean ground beef
1 onion, quartered
1 bunch scallions, chopped
3 garlic cloves, crushed
1 teaspoon ground nutmeg
1 tablespoon coriander seeds, dry-fried
   and ground
2 teaspoons cumin seeds, dry-fried
   and ground
4 eggs, beaten
oil for shallow-frying
salt and freshly ground black pepper

1 While the potatoes are still warm, mash them in the pan until they are well broken up. Add to the ground beef and mix well together.

2 Finely chop the onion, scallions and garlic. Add to the meat with the ground nutmeg, coriander and cumin. Stir in enough beaten egg to give a soft consistency which can be formed into fritters. Season to taste.

3 Heat the oil in a large frying pan. Using a dessertspoon, scoop out 6–8 oval-shaped fritters and drop them into the hot oil. Allow to set, so that they keep their shape (this will take about 3 minutes) and then turn over and cook for another minute.

4 Drain well on paper towels and keep warm while cooking the remaining fritters.

Barbecued Pork Spareribs

INGREDIENTS

Serves 4

2 ¼ pounds pork spareribs
1 onion
2 garlic cloves
1 inch fresh ginger root
⅓ cup dark soy sauce
1–2 fresh red chilies, seeded
   and chopped
1 teaspoon tamarind pulp, soaked in
   ⅓ cup water
1–2 tablespoons dark brown sugar
2 tablespoons peanut oil
salt and freshly ground black pepper

1 Wipe the pork ribs and place them in a wok, wide frying pan or large flameproof casserole.

2 Finely chop the onion, crush the garlic and peel and slice the ginger. Blend the soy sauce, onion, garlic, ginger and chopped chilies together to a paste in a food processor or with a mortar and pestle. Strain the tamarind and reserve the juice. Add the tamarind juice, brown sugar, oil and seasoning to taste to the onion mixture and mix well together.

3 Pour the sauce over the ribs and toss well to coat. Bring to a boil and then simmer, uncovered and stirring frequently, for 30 minutes. Add extra water if necessary.

4 Put the ribs on a rack in a roasting pan, place under a preheated broiler, on a barbecue grill or in the oven at 400°F. Continue cooking until the ribs are tender, about 20 minutes, depending on the thickness of the ribs. Baste the ribs with the sauce and turn them over from time to time.

Balinese Spiced Duck

There is a delightful hotel on the beach at Sanur which cooks this delicious duck dish perfectly.

INGREDIENTS

Serves 4

8 duck portions, fat trimmed
    and reserved
¹/₄ cup dried coconut
³/₄ cup coconut milk
salt and freshly ground black pepper
Deep-fried Onions and salad leaves or
    fresh herb sprigs, to garnish

For the spice paste

1 small onion or 4–6 shallots, sliced
2 garlic cloves, sliced
½ inch fresh ginger root, peeled
    and sliced
½ inch fresh *laos*, peeled and sliced
1 inch fresh turmeric or
    ½ teaspoon ground turmeric
1–2 red chilies, seeded and sliced
4 macadamia nuts or 8 almonds
1 teaspoon coriander seeds, dry-fried

1 Place the duck fat trimmings in a heated frying pan, and render the fat over a low heat. Reserve the fat.

2 Dry-fry the dried coconut in a preheated pan until crisp and brown in color.

3 To make the spice paste, blend the onion or shallots, garlic, ginger, *laos*, fresh or ground turmeric, chilies, nuts and coriander seeds to a paste in a food processor or with a mortar and pestle.

4 Spread the spice paste over the duck portions and let marinate in a cool place for 3–4 hours. Preheat the oven to 325°F. Shake off and reserve the spice paste, then transfer the duck breasts to an oiled roasting pan. Cover with a double layer of foil and cook the duck breasts in the preheated oven for 2 hours.

5 Turn the oven temperature up to 375°F. Heat the reserved duck fat in a pan, add the spice paste and fry for 1–2 minutes. Stir in the coconut milk and simmer for 2 minutes. Discard the duck juices then cover the duck with the spice mixture and sprinkle with the toasted coconut. Cook in the oven for 20–30 minutes.

6 Arrange the duck on a warm serving platter and sprinkle with the Deep-fried Onions. Season to taste and serve with the salad leaves or fresh herb sprigs of your choice.

Duck with Chinese Mushrooms and Ginger

Ducks are often seen, comically herded in single file, along the water channels between the rice paddies throughout the country. The substantial Chinese population in Indonesia is particularly fond of duck and the delicious ingredients in this recipe give it an oriental flavor.

INGREDIENTS

Serves 4

5½-pound duck
1 teaspoon sugar
¼ cup light soy sauce
2 garlic cloves, crushed
8 dried Chinese mushrooms, soaked in
   1½ cups warm water for 15 minutes
1 onion, sliced
2 inches fresh ginger root, sliced and
   cut in matchsticks
7 ounces baby corn
3–4 scallions, white bulbs left whole,
   green tops sliced
1–2 tablespoons cornstarch, mixed to a
   paste with 4 tablespoons water
salt and freshly ground black pepper
boiled rice, to serve

1 Cut the duck along the breast, open it up and cut along each side of the backbone. Use the backbone, wings and giblets to make a stock, to use later in the recipe. Any trimmings of fat can be rendered in a frying pan, to use later in the recipe. Cut each leg and each breast in half. Place in a bowl, rub with the sugar and then pour over the soy sauce and garlic.

2 Strain the mushrooms, reserving the soaking liquid. Trim and discard the stalks.

3 Fry the onion and ginger in the duck fat, in a frying pan, until they give off a good aroma. Push to one side. Lift the duck pieces out of the soy sauce and fry them until browned. Add the mushrooms and reserved liquid.

4 Add 2½ cups of the duck stock or water to the browned duck pieces. Season, cover and cook over a gentle heat for about 1 hour, or until the duck is tender.

5 Add the corn and the white part of the scallions and cook for another 10 minutes. Remove from the heat and add the corn paste. Return to the heat and bring to a boil, stirring. Cook for about 1 minute until glossy. Sprinkle with the sliced scallion tops and serve with boiled rice.

VARIATION

Replace the corn with chopped celery and slices of drained, canned water chestnuts.

Spiced Chicken Sauté

Ingredients

Serves 4

3–3½-pound chicken, cut in 8 pieces
1 teaspoon each salt and freshly ground
    black pepper
2 garlic cloves, crushed
⅝ cup sunflower oil

For the sauce

2 tablespoons butter
2 tablespoons sunflower oil
1 onion, sliced
4 garlic cloves, crushed
2 large, ripe beefsteak tomatoes, sliced
    and chopped, or 14-ounce can
    chopped tomatoes with chili, drained
2½ cups water
¼ cup dark soy sauce
salt and freshly ground black pepper
sliced fresh red chili, to garnish
Deep-fried Onions, to
    garnish (optional)
boiled rice, to serve

1 Preheat the oven to 375°F. Make two slashes in the fleshy part of each chicken piece. Rub well with the salt, pepper and garlic. Drizzle with a little of the oil and bake for about 30 minutes, or shallow-fry in hot oil for 12–15 minutes, until brown.

2 To make the sauce, heat the butter and oil in a wok and fry the onion and garlic until soft. Add the tomatoes, water, soy sauce and seasoning. Boil briskly for 5 minutes to reduce the sauce and concentrate the flavor.

3 Add the chicken to the sauce in the wok. Turn the chicken pieces over in the sauce to coat them well. Continue cooking slowly for about 20 minutes until the chicken pieces are tender. Stir the mixture occasionally.

4 Arrange the chicken on a warm serving platter and garnish with the sliced chili and Deep-fried Onions, if using. Serve with boiled rice.

Stir-fried Chicken with Pineapple

Ingredients

Serves 4–6

1¼ pounds boneless, skinless chicken
    breasts, thinly sliced at an angle
2 tablespoons cornstarch
4 tablespoons sunflower oil
1 garlic clove, crushed
2 inches fresh ginger root, peeled and
    cut in matchsticks
1 small onion, thinly sliced
1 fresh pineapple, peeled, cored and
    cubed, or 15-ounce can pineapple
    chunks in natural juice
2 tablespoons dark soy sauce or
    1 tablespoon *kecap manis*
6–8 scallions, white bulbs left whole,
    green tops sliced
salt and freshly ground black pepper

1 Toss the strips of chicken in the cornstarch with a little seasoning. Fry in hot oil until tender.

2 Lift out of the wok or frying pan and keep warm. Reheat the oil and fry the garlic, ginger and onion until soft, but not browned. Add the fresh pineapple and ½ cup water, or the canned pineapple pieces together with their juice.

3 Stir in the soy sauce or *kecap manis* and return the chicken to the pan to heat through.

4 Taste and adjust the seasoning. Stir in the whole scallion bulbs and half of the sliced green tops. Toss well together and then turn the chicken stir-fry onto a serving platter. Serve garnished with the remaining sliced green scallions.

Spicy Meatballs

Serve *Pergedel Djawa* with either a *sambal* or spicy sauce.

INGREDIENTS

Makes 24

1 large onion, roughly chopped
1–2 fresh red chilies, seeded
  and chopped
2 garlic cloves, crushed
¼ teaspoon shrimp paste, prepared
1 tablespoon coriander seeds
1 teaspoon cumin seeds
1 pound lean ground beef
2 teaspoons dark soy sauce
1 teaspoon dark brown sugar
juice of ½ lemon
a little beaten egg
oil for shallow-frying
salt and freshly ground black pepper
fresh cilantro sprigs, to garnish

1 Put the onion, chilies, garlic and shrimp paste in a food processor. Process but do not over-chop or the onion will become too wet and spoil the consistency of the meatballs. Dry-fry the coriander and cumin seeds in a preheated pan for about 1 minute, to release the aroma. Do not brown. Grind with a mortar and pestle.

2 Put the meat in a large bowl. Stir in the onion mixture. Add the ground coriander and cumin, soy sauce, seasoning, sugar and lemon juice. Bind with a little beaten egg and shape into small, even-size balls.

3 Chill the meatballs briefly to firm them, if necessary. Fry in shallow oil, turning often, until cooked through and browned. This will take 4–5 minutes, depending on their size.

4 Remove from the pan, drain on paper towels and serve, garnished with cilantro sprigs.

Beef and Eggplant Curry

INGREDIENTS

Serves 6

½ cup sunflower oil
2 onions, thinly sliced
1 inch fresh ginger root, sliced and
    cut in matchsticks
1 garlic clove, crushed
2 fresh red chilies, seeded and very
    finely sliced
1 inch fresh turmeric, peeled and
    crushed, or 1 teaspoon
    ground turmeric
1 lemon grass stem, lower part finely
    sliced, top bruised
1½ pounds braising steak, cut in even-
    size strips
14 fluid-ounce can coconut milk
1¼ cups water
1 eggplant, sliced and patted dry
1 teaspoon tamarind pulp, soaked in
    4 tablespoons warm water
salt and freshly ground black pepper
finely sliced chili, (optional) and
    Deep-fried Onions, to garnish
boiled rice, to serve

1 Heat half the oil and fry the
onions, ginger and garlic until they
give off a rich aroma. Add the chilies,
turmeric and the lower part of the
lemon grass. Push to one side and then
turn up the heat and add the steak,
stirring until the meat changes color.

COOK'S TIP

If you want to make this curry, *Gulai
Terung Dengan Daging,* ahead, prepare to
the end of step 2 and finish later.

2 Add the coconut milk, water,
lemon grass top and seasoning to
taste. Cover and simmer gently for
1½ hours, or until the meat is tender.

3 Towards the end of the cooking
time heat the remaining oil in a
frying pan. Fry the eggplant slices until
brown on both sides.

4 Add the browned eggplant slices to
the beef curry and cook for
another 15 minutes. Stir gently from
time to time. Strain the tamarind and
stir the juice into the curry. Taste and
adjust the seasoning. Put into a warm
serving dish. Garnish with the sliced
chili, if using, and Deep-fried Onions,
and serve with boiled rice.

SAMBALS AND PICKLES

A sambal or sambalan is a sauce or dip that is placed on the table to give extra flavor to a saté. Sambal Kecap or Chili Sambal can be used to pep up soups and is used in making spice pastes. Sambal Goreng is a chili-spiced sauce to which coconut cream is added. A few minutes before serving, a variety of cooked ingredients, from shrimp to chicken livers, hard-boiled eggs or vegetables, are added to the sauce. It is a really useful basic sauce, rather like our tomato or cheese sauces, which can be used to dress up different ingredients in a variety of ways. Acar or atjar is a side dish with either a sweet-sour or a turmeric-based dressing, not unlike a piccalilli.

Sambal Kecap

This can be served as a dip for *satés* instead of the usual peanut sauce and is particularly good with beef and chicken *satés* and deep-fried chicken.

INGREDIENTS

Makes about ⅝ cup
1 fresh red chili, seeded and
   finely chopped
2 garlic cloves, crushed
4 tablespoons dark soy sauce
4 teaspoons lemon juice, or 1–1½
   tablespoons prepared tamarind juice
2 tablespoons hot water
2 tablespoons Deep-fried
   Onions (optional)

1 Mix the chili, garlic, soy sauce, lemon or tamarind juice and hot water together in a bowl.

2 Stir in the Deep-fried Onions, if using, and leave to stand for 30 minutes before serving.

Deep-fried Onions

Known as *Bawang Goreng,* these are a traditional garnish and accompaniment to many Indonesian dishes. Asian stores sell them ready-made, but it is simple to make them at home, using fresh onions, or for an even faster way, use an 2–3-ounce package of freeze-dried onions, which you can fry in about 1 cup of sunflower oil. This gives you 4 ounces of fried onion flakes. The small red onions that can be bought in Asian shops are excellent when deep-fried as they contain less water than most European varieties.

INGREDIENTS

Makes 1 pound
1 pound onions
oil for deep-frying

1 Peel and slice the onions as evenly and finely as possible.

2 Spread out thinly on paper towels, in an airy place, and leave to dry for 30 minutes to 2 hours.

3 Heat the oil in deep-fryer or wok to 375°F. Fry the onions in batches, until crisp and golden, turning all the time. Drain well on paper towels and cool. Deep-fried Onions may be stored in an airtight container.

COOK'S TIP

Garlic can be prepared and cooked in the same way, or some can be fried with the last batch of onions. Deep-fried Garlic gives an added dimension in flavor as a garnish for many dishes.

Sambal Goreng

Traditional flavorings for this dish are fine strips of calves' liver, chicken livers, green beans or hard-boiled eggs. A westernized version is shown here.

INGREDIENTS

Makes 3¹/₄ cups

1 teaspoon shrimp paste
2 onions, quartered
2 garlic cloves, crushed
1 inch fresh *laos*, peeled
   and sliced
2 teaspoons Chili Sambal or 2 fresh red
   chilies, seeded and sliced
¼ teaspoon salt
2 tablespoons oil
3 tablespoons tomato paste
2½ cups broth or water
4 tablespoons tamarind juice
pinch sugar
3 tablespoons coconut milk or cream

1 Grind the shrimp paste, with the onions and garlic, to a paste in a food processor or with a mortar and pestle. Add the *laos*, Chili Sambal or sliced chilies and salt. Process or pound to a fine paste.

2 Fry the paste in hot oil for 2 minutes, without browning, until the mixture gives off a rich aroma.

3 Add the tomato paste and the broth or water and cook for about 10 minutes. Add 12 ounces cooked chicken pieces and 2 ounces cooked and sliced French beans, or one of the flavoring variations below, to half the quantity of the sauce. Cook in the sauce for 3–4 minutes, then stir in the tamarind juice, sugar and coconut milk or cream at the last minute, before tasting and serving.

--- VARIATIONS ---

Tomato *Sambal Goreng* – Add 1 pound of peeled, seeded and coarsely chopped tomatoes, before the broth.

Shrimp *Sambal Goreng* – Add 12 ounces cooked, peeled shrimp and 1 green bell pepper, seeded and chopped.

Egg *Sambal Goreng* – Add 3 or 4 hard-boiled eggs, shelled and chopped, and 2 tomatoes, peeled, seeded and chopped.

Mixed Vegetable Pickle

If you can obtain fresh turmeric, it makes such a difference to the color and appearance of *Acar Campur*. You can use almost any vegetable, bearing in mind that you need a balance of textures, flavors and colors.

INGREDIENTS

Makes 2–3 11-ounce jars

1 fresh red chili, seeded and sliced
1 onion, quartered
2 garlic cloves, crushed
½ teaspoon shrimp paste
4 macadamia nuts or 8 almonds
1 inch fresh turmeric, peeled and
   sliced, or 1 teaspoon ground turmeric
¼ cup sunflower oil
2 cups white vinegar
1 cup water
3–6 tablespoons granulated sugar
3 carrots
8 ounces green beans
1 small cauliflower
1 cucumber
8 ounces white cabbage
¾ cup dry-roasted peanuts,
   roughly crushed
salt

1 Place the chili, onion, garlic, shrimp paste, nuts and turmeric in a food processor and blend to a paste, or pound in a mortar with a pestle.

2 Heat the oil and stir-fry the paste to release the aroma. Add the vinegar, water, sugar and salt. Bring to a boil. Simmer for 10 minutes.

3 Cut the carrots into flower shapes. Cut the green beans into short, neat lengths. Separate the cauliflower into neat, bite-size florets. Peel and seed the cucumber and cut the flesh in neat, bite-size pieces. Cut the cabbage in neat, bite-size pieces.

4 Blanch each vegetable separately, in a large pan of boiling water, for 1 minute. Transfer to a colander and rinse with cold water, to halt the cooking. Drain well.

--- COOK'S TIP ---

This pickle is even better if you make it a few days ahead.

5 Add the vegetables to the sauce. Slowly bring to a boil and allow to cook for 5–10 minutes. Do not overcook – the vegetables should still be crunchy.

6 Add the peanuts and cool. Spoon into clean jars with lids.

Tomato Sambal

Sambal Tomaat, from Surabaya, can be used as a dip to eat with fritters and snack foods.

INGREDIENTS

Makes about 1¼ cups
2 large beefsteak tomatoes, about 14 ounces in all, peeled if liked
1 fresh red chili, seeded, or ½ teaspoon chili powder
2–3 garlic cloves
4 tablespoons dark brown sugar
3 tablespoons sunflower oil
1 tablespoon lime or lemon juice
salt

1 Cut the tomatoes in quarters and remove the cores. Place in a food processor with the chili or chili powder, garlic, sugar and salt to taste. Process to a purée.

2 Fry the tomato pureé in hot oil, stirring all the time, until the mixture thickens and has lost its raw taste. Add the lime or lemon juice. Cool, then season. Serve warm or cold.

Carrot and Apple Salad

Known as *Selada Bortel*, this simple, crunchy salad is always a perfect accompaniment to spicy Indonesian food. It's best to grate the apple at the last minute and sprinkle it liberally with lemon juice to prevent discoloration. Cover the salad with plastic wrap and store in the fridge until needed.

1 Coarsely grate the carrot and set aside. Grate the apple, including the skin, and drizzle it with the lemon juice to prevent discoloration. Mix gently with your hand to evenly coat the apple with the lemon juice.

2 Add the sunflower oil and sugar to the apple mixture. Season to taste with salt and black pepper, then stir in the grated carrot.

3 Cover the salad with plastic wrap and chill in the fridge for a short time, until required.

INGREDIENTS

Serves 6
3 large carrots
1 green apple
juice of 1 lemon
3 tablespoons sunflower oil
1 teaspoon sugar
salt and freshly ground black pepper

VARIATION

For a tangy flavor, add lime juice and a little grated lime rind to the apple.

Sweet and Sour Fruit and Vegetable Salad

Acar Bening makes a perfect accompaniment to many spicy dishes, with its clean taste and bright, jewel-like colors. Any leftover salad can be covered and stored in the fridge for up to two days. This is an essential dish for buffets when it will be enough for about eight servings.

INGREDIENTS

Serves 8

1 small cucumber

1 onion, thinly sliced and sprinkled with salt

1 small, ripe pineapple or 15-ounce can pineapple rings

1 green bell pepper, seeded and thinly sliced

3 firm tomatoes, cut in wedges

1 ounce golden granulated sugar

3–4 tablespoons cider or white wine vinegar

½ cup water

salt

1 Peel the cucumber and cut in half lengthways. Remove the seeds with a small spoon. Cut the cucumber in even-size pieces. Sprinkle with a little salt. Rinse and dry the onion and place in a large bowl. Rinse the cucumber and pat dry, then add to the onion in the bowl.

2 Peel the fresh pineapple, if using, removing all the eyes by cutting them out from top to bottom. Slice the pineapple thinly, then core the slices and cut in neat pieces. If using canned pineapple rings, cut in similarly sized pieces. Add them to the bowl together with the bell pepper and tomatoes.

3 Heat the sugar, vinegar and water until the sugar dissolves. Remove from the heat and leave to cool. When cold, add a little salt to taste and then pour over the fruit and vegetables. Cover and chill until required.

— VARIATION —

To make an Indonesian-style Cucumber Salad, prepare a whole cucumber as in the above recipe. Make half the dressing and pour over the cucumber. Add a few chopped scallions. Cover and chill. Serve sprinkled with toasted sesame seeds.

Chili Sambal

Sambal Ulek will keep for several weeks in a well-sealed jar in the fridge, so it is worth making up the whole or half of the quantity at a time. Use a stainless steel or plastic spoon to measure it out. This sauce is fiercely hot and, should you get any on your fingers, wash them well in soapy water *immediately*.

INGREDIENTS

Makes 1 pound

1 pound fresh red chilies, seeded

2 teaspoons salt

1 Plunge the chilies into a pan of boiling water and cook them for 5–8 minutes. Drain and then grind in a food processor, without making the paste too smooth.

2 Turn into a screw-topped glass jar, stir in the salt and cover with a piece of wax paper or plastic wrap. Screw on the lid and store in the fridge. Spoon into small dishes to serve as an accompaniment or use in recipes as suggested.

RICE AND NOODLES

Rice is served in Indonesia at least once, and more often twice, a day. Even today, many people from the city will return home to help their families and neighbors with the rice harvest. Lebaran, *the feast day to celebrate the end of Ramadan, is the time when all families come together and a huge, cone-shaped mound of* Nasi Kuning *or Festive Rice, is the centerpiece of the table.*

Noodles, mee, *reflect the Chinese influence on Indonesian cuisine and variations of these recipes will be found in many neighboring countries.*

Noodles, Chicken and Shrimp in Coconut Broth

INGREDIENTS

Serves 8

2 onions, quartered
1 inch fresh ginger root, sliced
2 garlic cloves
4 macadamia nuts or 8 almonds
1–2 fresh chilies, seeded and sliced
2 lemon grass stems, lower
  2 inches sliced
2 inches fresh turmeric, peeled and
  sliced, or 1 teaspoon ground turmeric
1 tablespoon coriander seeds, dry-fried
1 teaspoon cumin seeds, dry-fried
4 tablespoons sunflower oil
14-fluid ounce can coconut milk
6¼ cups broth
13-ounce package rice noodles, soaked
  in cold water
12 ounces cooked large shrimp
salt and freshly ground black pepper

For the garnishes
4 hard-boiled eggs
8 ounces cooked chicken, chopped
8 ounces bean sprouts
1 bunch scallions, shredded
Deep-fried Onions

1 Place the quartered onions, ginger, garlic and nuts in a food processor, with the chilies, sliced lemon grass, and turmeric. Process to a paste. Alternatively, pound all the ingredients with a mortar and pestle. Grind the coriander and cumin seeds coarsely and add to the paste.

2 Heat the oil in a pan and fry the spice paste, without coloring, to bring out the flavors. Add the coconut milk, broth and seasoning. Simmer for 5–10 minutes, while preparing the noodles and garnishes.

3 Drain the noodles and plunge them into a large pan of salted, boiling water for 2 minutes. Remove from the heat and drain in a colander. Rinse well with plenty of cold water, to halt the cooking. Add the large shrimp to the soup just before serving and heat through for a minute or two.

4 Shell the hard-boiled eggs and cut into quarters. Arrange the garnishes in separate bowls. Each person helps themselves to noodles, tops them with soup, eggs, chicken or bean sprouts then scatters shredded scallions and the Deep-fried Onions on top.

Compressed Rice Shapes

INGREDIENTS

Serves 4 – 8

2 x 4-ounce packages boil-in-the-
  bag rice
salt

> ——— COOK'S TIP ———
>
> For the best results for *Longtong,* use boil-in-the-bag rice that is not marked as par-boiled. The grains need to compress and stick together to make the rice cakes, and par-boiled rice grains remain too separate. Otherwise use Basmati or Thai fragrant rice and wrap in cheesecloth bags or foil. Traditionally, these packets are made from banana leaves or woven coconut fronds.

1 Place the bags of rice in a large pan of salted, boiling water and cook for 1¼ hours, or until the rice is cooked and fills all the bag like a plump pillow. The bags must be covered with water throughout; use an old saucer or plate to weigh them down.

2 Lift out the bags of rice, drain and set aside to cool completely, before stripping off the bags.

3 With a sharp, wetted knife, cut into neat cubes or slices and then into diamond shapes. Serve with *satés.*

Festive Rice

Nasi Kuning is served at special events – weddings, birthdays or farewell parties.

Ingredients

Serves 8

1 pound Thai fragrant rice
4 tablespoons oil
2 garlic cloves, crushed
2 onions, finely sliced
2 inches fresh turmeric, peeled and crushed
3 cups water
14-fluid ounce can coconut milk
1–2 lemon grass stems, bruised
1–2 *pandan* leaves (optional)
salt

For the accompaniments

omelet strips
2 fresh red chilies, shredded
cucumber chunks
tomato wedges
Deep-fried Onions
Coconut and Peanut Relish (optional)
Shrimp Crackers

1 Wash the rice in several changes of water. Drain well.

2 Heat the oil in a wok and gently fry the crushed garlic, the finely sliced onions and the crushed fresh turmeric for a few minutes until soft but not browned.

COOK'S TIP

It is the custom to shape the rice into a cone (to represent a volcano) and then surround with the accompaniments. Shape with oiled hands or use a conical strainer.

3 Add the rice and and stir well so that each grain is thoroughly coated. Pour in the water and coconut milk and add the lemon grass, *pandan* leaves, if using, and salt.

4 Bring to a boil, stirring well. Cover and cook gently for about 15–20 minutes, until all of the liquid has been absorbed.

5 Remove from the heat. Cover with a dish towel, put on the lid and let stand in a warm place for 15 minutes. Remove the lemon grass and *pandan* leaves.

6 Turn onto a serving platter and garnish with the accompaniments.

Nasi Goreng

One of the most familiar and well-known Indonesian dishes. This is a marvelous way to use up leftover rice, chicken and meats such as pork. It is important that the rice is really cold and the grains separate before adding the other ingredients, so it's best to cook the rice the day before.

INGREDIENTS

Serves 4–6

1⅞ cup long grain rice, such as basmati, cooked and allowed to become completely cold
2 eggs
2 tablespoons water
7 tablespoons oil
8 ounces pork loin or tenderloin of beef
4 ounces cooked, peeled shrimp
6–8 ounces cooked chicken, chopped
2–3 fresh red chilies, seeded and sliced
½ teaspoon shrimp paste
2 garlic cloves, crushed
1 onion, sliced
2 tablespoons dark soy sauce or 3–4 tablespoons tomato ketchup
salt and freshly ground black pepper
celery leaves, Deep-fried Onions and cilantro sprigs, to garnish

1 Once the rice is cooked and cooled, fork it through to separate the grains and keep it in a covered pan or dish until required.

2 Beat the eggs with seasoning and the water and make two or three omelets in a frying pan, with a minimum of oil. Roll up each omelet and cut in strips when cold. Set aside.

3 Cut the pork or beef into neat strips and put the meat, shrimp and chicken pieces in separate bowls. Shred one of the chilies and reserve it.

4 Put the shrimp paste, with the remaining chili, garlic and onion, in a food processor and grind to a fine paste. Alternatively, pound together using a mortar and pestle.

5 Fry the paste in the remaining hot oil, without browning, until it gives off a rich, spicy aroma. Add the pork or beef, tossing the meat constantly, to seal in the juices. Cook for 2 minutes, stirring constantly. Add the shrimp , cook for 2 minutes and then stir in the chicken, cold rice, dark soy sauce or ketchup and seasoning to taste. Stir constantly to prevent the rice from sticking.

6 Turn onto a hot platter and garnish with the omelet strips, celery leaves, onions, reserved shredded chili and the cilantro sprigs.

Coconut Rice

This is a very popular way of cooking rice throughout the whole of South-east Asia. *Nasi Uduk* makes a wonderful accompaniment to any dish, and goes particularly well with fish, chicken and pork.

INGREDIENTS

Serves 4–6
1⅞ cups Thai fragrant rice
14-fluid ounce can coconut milk
1¼ cups water
½ teaspoon ground coriander
1 cinnamon stick
1 lemon grass stem, bruised
1 *pandan* or bay leaf (optional)
salt
Deep-fried Onions, to garnish

1 Wash the rice in several changes of water and then put in a pan with the coconut milk, water, coriander, cinnamon stick, lemon grass and *pandan* or bay leaf, if using, and salt. Bring to a boil, stirring to prevent the rice from settling on the bottom of the pan. Cover and cook over a very low heat for 12–15 minutes, or until all the coconut milk has been absorbed.

2 Fork the rice through carefully and remove the cinnamon stick, lemon grass and *pandan* or bay leaf. Cover the pan with a tight-fitting lid and then cook over the lowest possible heat for another 3–5 minutes.

3 Pile the rice onto a warm serving dish and serve garnished with the crisp Deep-fried Onions.

Rice Porridge with Chicken

Bubur Ayam is a dish which turns up all over the East, often served as sustaining breakfast fare. It can be served very simply, with just the chicken stirred into it. Hearty eaters tuck into helpings of porridge drizzled with a little soy sauce, with strips of chicken, shrimps, Deep-fried Onions, garlic and strips of fresh chili, topped with a lightly fried egg and garnished with celery leaves.

INGREDIENTS

Serves 6
2¼-pound chicken, cut in 4 pieces, or
    4 chicken quarters
7½ cups water
1 large onion, quartered
1 inch fresh ginger root, peeled, halved
    and bruised
1⅞ cups Thai fragrant rice, rinsed
salt and freshly ground black pepper

1 Place the chicken pieces in a large pan with the water, onion quarters and ginger. Add seasoning, bring to a boil and simmer for 45–50 minutes, until the chicken is tender. Remove from the heat. Lift out the chicken, remove the meat and discard the skin and bones. Cut the chicken into bite-size pieces. Reserve the stock.

2 Strain the chicken stock into a clean pan and make it up to 7½ cups with water.

3 Add the rinsed rice to the chicken stock and stir continuously until it comes to a boil, to prevent the rice from settling on the bottom of the pan. Simmer gently for 20 minutes, without a lid. Stir, cover and cook the rice for 20 minutes more, stirring from time to time until the rice is soft and rather like a creamy risotto.

4 Stir the chicken pieces into the porridge and heat through for 5 minutes. Serve as it is, or with any of the garnishes and accompaniments suggested in the introduction.

Noodles with Meatballs

Mie Rebus is a one-pot meal, for which the East is renowned.

INGREDIENTS

Serves 6

1 pound Spicy Meatball mixture
12 ounces dried egg noodles
3 tablespoons sunflower oil
1 large onion, finely sliced
2 garlic cloves, crushed
1 inch fresh ginger root, peeled and cut in thin matchsticks
5 cups broth
2 tablespoons dark soy sauce
2 celery stalks, finely sliced, leaves reserved
6 Chinese cabbage leaves, cut in bite-size pieces
1 handful snow peas, cut in strips
salt and freshly ground black pepper

1 Prepare the meatballs, making them quite small. Set aside.

2 Add the noodles to a large pan of salted, boiling water and stir so that the noodles do not settle at the bottom. Simmer for 3–4 minutes, or until *al dente*. Drain in a colander and rinse with plenty of cold water. Set aside.

3 Heat the oil in a wide pan and fry the onion, garlic and ginger until soft but not browned. Add the broth and soy sauce and bring to a boil.

4 Add the meatballs, half-cover and allow to simmer until they are cooked, about 5–8 minutes depending on size. Just before serving, add the sliced celery and, after 2 minutes, add the Chinese cabbage and snow peas. Taste and adjust the seasoning.

5 Divide the noodles among soup bowls, add the meatballs and vegetables and pour the soup on top. Garnish with the reserved celery leaves.

Bamie Goreng

This fried noodle dish is wonderfully accommodating. To the basic recipe you can add other vegetables, such as mushrooms, tiny pieces of chayote, broccoli, leeks or beansprouts, if you prefer. As with fried rice, you can use whatever you have to hand, bearing in mind the need to achieve a balance of colors, flavors and textures.

INGREDIENTS

Serves 6–8
1 pound dried egg noodles
1 boneless, skinless chicken breast
4 ounces pork loin
4 ounces calves' liver (optional)
2 eggs, beaten
6 tablespoons oil
2 tablespoons butter or margarine
2 garlic cloves, crushed
4 ounces cooked, peeled shrimp
4 ounces spinach or Chinese cabbage
2 celery stalks, finely sliced
4 scallions, shredded
about 4 tablespoons chicken broth
dark soy sauce and light soy sauce
salt and freshly ground black pepper
Deep-fried Onions and celery leaves, to garnish
Sweet and Sour Fruit and Vegetable Salad, to serve (optional)

2 Finely slice the chicken, pork loin and calves' liver, if using.

1 Cook the noodles in salted, boiling water for 3–4 minutes. Drain, rinse with cold water and drain again. Set aside until required.

3 Season the eggs. Heat 1 teaspoon oil with the butter or margarine in a small pan until melted and then stir in the eggs and keep stirring until scrambled. Set aside.

4 Heat the remaining oil in a wok and fry the garlic with the chicken, pork and liver for 2–3 minutes, until they have changed color. Add the shrimp, spinach or Chinese cabbage, celery and scallions, tossing well.

5 Add the cooked and drained noodles and toss well again so that all the ingredients are well mixed. Add enough broth just to moisten and dark and light soy sauce to taste. Finally, stir in the scrambled eggs.

6 Garnish the dish with Deep-fried Onions and celery leaves. Serve with Sweet and Sour Fruit and Vegetable Salad, if using.

VEGETABLES AND SALADS

Gado-Gado, *along with* satés *and* Rendang, *has gained an international reputation — and rightly so. Presentation is all important — try serving a platter of the lightly blanched vegetables or fruit and raw vegetables, each with peanut sauce, as a stunning lunch dish. Other vegetables, from Stir-fried Greens and the delicious Spiced Cauliflower Braise to the steamed Zucchini with Noodles dish, illustrate the rich variety of vegetarian-style Indonesian recipes that are on hand to tempt you.*

Spiced Cauliflower Braise

A delicious vegetable stew, known as *Sambal Kol Kembang,* which combines coconut milk with spices and is perfect as a vegetarian main course or as part of a buffet.

INGREDIENTS

Serves 4

1 cauliflower
2 medium or 1 large tomato(es)
1 onion, chopped
2 garlic cloves, crushed
1 fresh green chili, seeded
½ tablespoon ground turmeric
½ teaspoon shrimp paste
2 tablespoons sunflower oil
14-fluid ounce can coconut milk
1 cup water
1 teaspoon sugar
1 teaspoon tamarind pulp, soaked in
  3 tablespoons warm water
salt

1 Trim the stalk from the cauliflower and divide into tiny florets. Skin the tomato(es) if liked. Chop the flesh into ½–1-inch pieces.

2 Grind the chopped onion, garlic, green chili, ground turmeric and shrimp paste together to a paste in a food processor or with a mortar and pestle. Heat the sunflower oil in a wok or large frying pan and fry the spice paste to bring out the aromatic flavors, without allowing it to brown.

3 Add the cauliflower florets and toss well to coat in the spices. Stir in the coconut milk, water, sugar and salt to taste. Simmer for 5 minutes. Strain the tamarind and reserve the juice.

4 Add the tamarind juice and chopped tomatoes to the pan then cook for 2–3 minutes only. Taste for check the seasoning and serve.

Spicy Scrambled Eggs

This is a lovely way to liven up scrambled eggs. When making *Orak Arik,* prepare all the ingredients ahead so that the vegetables retain all their crunch and color.

INGREDIENTS

Serves 4

2 tablespoons sunflower oil
1 onion, finely sliced
8 ounces Chinese cabbage, finely sliced
  or cut in diamonds
7-ounce can corn kernels
1 small fresh red chili, seeded and finely
  sliced (optional)
2 tablespoons water
2 eggs, beaten
salt and freshly ground black pepper
Deep-fried Onions, to garnish

1 Heat a wok, add the oil and fry the onion, until soft but not browned.

2 Add the Chinese cabbage and toss well together. Add the corn, chili and water. Cover with a lid and cook for 2 minutes.

3 Remove the lid and stir in the beaten eggs and the seasoning. Stir constantly until the eggs are creamy and just set. Serve on warmed plates, sprinkled with crisp Deep-fried Onions.

Tomato and Onion Salad

A refreshing salad, *Atjar Ketimun,* which can be made ahead; it improves if well chilled before serving. Use firm, slightly under-ripe tomatoes so the flesh does not collapse when cut into dice.

INGREDIENTS

Serves 6

1 cucumber
3 tablespoons good-quality rice- or white-wine vinegar
2 teaspoons sugar
1 tomato, skinned, seeded and diced
1 small onion, finely sliced
1 fresh red chili, seeded and chopped
salt

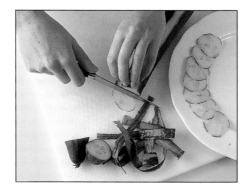

1 Trim the ends from the cucumber. Peel it lengthwise but leave some of the skin on, to make the salad look more attractive. Cut it in thin slices and lay them out on a large plate. Sprinkle with a little salt and set aside for 15 minutes. Rinse well and dry.

2 Mix the vinegar, sugar and a pinch of salt together. Arrange all the vegetables in a bowl and pour over the vinegar, sugar and salt mixture. Cover the salad and chill before serving.

Coconut and Peanut Relish

The aroma of toasted coconut is wonderful and will immediately have you dreaming of warmer climes! *Serudeng* is served as an accompaniment to many Indonesian dishes; any leftovers can be stored in an airtight tin.

INGREDIENTS

Serves 6–8

14 ounces fresh coconut, grated, or dried coconut
1 cup salted peanuts
¼ teaspoon shrimp paste
1 small onion, quartered
2–3 garlic cloves, crushed
3 tablespoons oil
½ teaspoon tamarind pulp, soaked in 2 tablespoons warm water
1 teaspoon coriander seeds, dry-fried and ground
½ teaspoon cumin seeds, dry-fried and ground
1 teaspoon dark brown sugar

1 Dry-fry the coconut in a wok or large frying pan over a medium heat, turning *all the time*, until it is crisp and a rich, golden color. Allow to cool and add half to the peanuts. Toss together to mix.

2 Grind the shrimp paste, with the onion and garlic, to a paste in a food processor or with a mortar and pestle. Fry in hot oil, without browning. Strain the tamarind and reserve the juice. Add the coriander, cumin, tamarind juice and brown sugar to the fried paste. Cook the mixture for 2–3 minutes, stirring constantly.

3 Stir in the remaining toasted coconut and let cool. When quite cold, mix with the peanut and coconut mixture.

Bean Curd and Cucumber Salad

Tahu Goreng Ketjap is a nutritious and refreshing salad with a hot, sweet and sour dressing. It is ideal for buffets.

INGREDIENTS

Serves 4–6
1 small cucumber
oil for frying
1 square fresh or 4 ounces long-life
   bean curd
4 ounces bean sprouts, trimmed
   and rinsed
salt

For the dressing
1 small onion, grated
2 garlic cloves, crushed
1–1½ teaspoons Chili Sambal
2–3 tablespoons dark soy sauce
1–2 tablespoons rice-wine vinegar
2 teaspoon dark brown sugar
salt
celery leaves, to garnish

1 Trim the ends from the cucumber and then cut it in neat cubes. Sprinkle with salt and set aside, while preparing the remaining ingredients.

--- COOK'S TIP ---

Bean sprouts come from the mung bean and are easily grown at home on damp cotton or in a plastic bean sprouter. They must be eaten when absolutely fresh, so when buying from a shop check that they are crisp and are not beginning to go brown or soft. Eat within a day or two.

2 Heat a little oil in a pan and fry the bean curd on both sides until golden brown. Drain on paper towels and cut in cubes.

3 Prepare the dressing by blending together the onion, garlic and Chili Sambal. Stir in the soy sauce, vinegar, sugar and salt to taste. You can do this in a screw-top glass jar.

4 Just before serving, rinse the cucumber under cold running water. Drain and dry thoroughly. Toss the cucumber, bean curd and bean prouts together in a serving bowl and pour over the dressing. Garnish with the celery leaves and serve the salad at once.

Stir-fried Greens

Quail's eggs look very attractive in *Chah Kang Kung*, but you can substitute some baby corn, halved at an angle.

INGREDIENTS

Serves 4

2 bunches spinach or chard or 1 head Chinese cabbage
3 garlic cloves, crushed
2 inches fresh ginger root, peeled and cut in matchsticks
3–4 tablespoons peanut oil
14 ounces boneless, skinless chicken breast, or pork loin, or a mixture of both, very finely sliced
12 quail's eggs, hard-boiled and shelled
1 fresh red chili, seeded and shredded
2–3 tablespoons oyster sauce
1 tablespoon brown sugar
2 teaspoons cornstarch, mixed with ¼ cup cold water
salt

— COOK'S TIP —

As with all stir-fries, don't start cooking until you have prepared all the ingredients and arranged them to hand. Cut everything into small, even-size pieces so the food can be cooked very quickly and all the colors and flavors preserved.

1 Wash the chosen leaves well and shake them dry. Strip the tender leaves from the stems and tear them into pieces. Discard the lower, tougher part of the stems and slice the remainder evenly.

2 Fry the garlic and ginger in the hot oil, without browning, for a minute. Add the chicken and/or pork and keep stirring it in the wok until the meat changes color. When the meat looks cooked, add the sliced stems first and cook them quickly; then add the torn leaves, quail's eggs and chili. Spoon in the oyster sauce and a little boiling water, if necessary. Cover and cook for 1–2 minutes only.

3 Remove the lid, stir and add sugar and salt to taste. Stir in the cornstarch and water mixture and toss thoroughly. Cook until the mixture is well coated in a glossy sauce.

4 Serve immediately, while still very hot and the colors are bright and glowingly jewel-like.

Indonesian Potatoes with Onions and Chili Sauce

This adds another dimension to French fries, with the addition of crisply fried onions and a spicy soy sauce and chili dressing. Eat *Kentang Gula* hot, warm or cold, as a tasty snack.

INGREDIENTS

Serves 6
3 large potatoes, about 8 ounces each, peeled and cut for fries
sunflower or peanut oil for deep-frying
2 onions, finely sliced
salt

For the dressing
1–2 fresh red chilies, seeded and ground, or ½ teaspoon Chili Sambal
3 tablespoons dark soy sauce

1 Rinse the potatoes and then thoroughly pat dry with paper towels. Heat the oil and deep-fry the potatoes, until they are golden brown in color and crisp.

2 Put the potatoes in a dish, sprinkle with salt and keep warm. Fry the onion slices in the hot oil until they are similarly crisp and golden brown. Drain well on paper towels and then add to the potatoes.

3 Mix the chilies or Chili Sambal with the soy sauce and heat gently.

4 Pour over the potato and onion mixture and serve as suggested.

VARIATION

Alternatively, boil the potatoes in their skins. Drain, cool, peel and slice them, then shallow-fry until golden. Cook the onions and pour over the dressing.

Zucchini with Noodles

Any zucchini or member of the squash family can be used in *Oseng Oseng,* which is reminiscent of a similar dish eaten in Malaysia, whose cuisine has strong links with Indonesia.

INGREDIENTS

Serves 4–6
1 pound zucchini, sliced
1 onion, finely sliced
1 garlic clove, finely chopped
2 tablespoons sunflower oil
½ teaspoon ground turmeric
2 tomatoes, chopped
3 tablespoons water
14 ounces cooked, peeled shrimp (optional)
1 ounce cellophane noodles
salt

1 Use a vegetable peeler to cut thin strips from the outside of each zucchini. Cut the strips in neat slices. Set the zucchini on one side. Fry the onion and garlic in hot oil; do not allow to brown.

2 Add the turmeric, zucchini slices, chopped tomatoes, water and shrimp, if using.

3 Put the noodles in a pan and pour over boiling water to cover, let stand for a minute and then drain. Cut the noodles in 2-inch lengths and add to the vegetables.

4 Cover with a lid and cook in their own steam for 2–3 minutes. Toss everything well together. Season with salt to taste and serve while still hot.

Cooked Vegetable Gado-Gado

Instead of putting everything on a large platter, you can serve individual servings of this salad. It is a perfect recipe for lunchtime or informal gatherings.

INGREDIENTS

Serves 6

8 ounces waxy potatoes, cooked
1 pound mixed cabbage, spinach and
    bean sprouts, in equal proportions,
    rinsed and shredded
½ cucumber, cut in wedges, salted and
    set aside for 15 minutes
2–3 eggs, hard-boiled and shelled
4 ounces fresh bean curd
oil for frying
6–8 large Shrimp Crackers
lemon juice
Deep-fried Onions, to garnish
Peanut Sauce, to serve

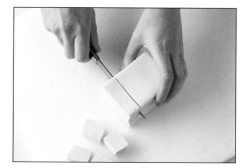

1 Cube the potatoes and set aside. Bring a large pan of salted water to a boil. Plunge one type of raw vegetable at a time into the pan for just a few seconds to blanch. Lift out the vegetables with a large slotted spoon or sieve and run under very cold water, or plunge them into iced water and set aside 2 minutes. Drain thoroughly. Blanch all the vegetables, except the cucumber, in this way.

2 Rinse the cucumber pieces and drain them well. Cut the eggs in quarters. Cut the bean curd into cubes.

3 Fry the bean curd in hot oil in a wok until crisp on both sides. Lift out and drain on paper towels.

4 Add more oil to the pan and then deep-fry the Shrimp Crackers one or two at a time. Reserve them on a tray lined with paper towels.

5 Arrange all the cooked vegetables attractively on a platter, with the cucumber, hard-boiled eggs and bean curd. Scatter with the lemon juice and Deep-fried Onions at the last minute.

6 Serve with the prepared Peanut Sauce and hand round the fried Shrimp Crackers separately.

Fruit and Raw Vegetable Gado-Gado

A banana leaf, which can be bought from oriental stores, can be used to line the platter for a special occasion.

INGREDIENTS

Serves 6

2 unripe pears, peeled at the last moment, or 6-ounce wedge *bangkuang* (yambean), peeled and cut in matchsticks
1–2 eating apples
juice of ½ lemon
1 small, crisp lettuce, shredded
½ cucumber, seeded, sliced and salted, set aside for 15 minutes, then rinsed and drained
6 small tomatoes, cut in wedges
3 slices fresh pineapple, cored and cut in wedges
3 eggs or 12 quail's eggs, hard-boiled and shelled
6 ounces egg noodles, cooked, cooled and chopped
Deep-fried Onions, to garnish

Peanut Sauce

2–4 fresh red chilies, seeded and ground, or 1 tablespoon Chili Sambal
1¼ cups coconut milk
12 ounces crunchy peanut butter
1 tablespoon dark soy sauce or dark brown sugar
1 teaspoon tamarind pulp, soaked in 3 tablespoons warm water, strained and juice reserved
coarsely crushed peanuts
salt

1 To make the Peanut Sauce, put the chilies or Chili Sambal and coconut milk in a pan. Add the peanut butter and heat gently, stirring, until no lumps of peanut butter remain.

2 Allow to simmer gently until the sauce thickens, then add the soy sauce or sugar and tamarind juice. Season with salt to taste. Pour into a bowl and sprinkle with a few coarsely crushed peanuts.

3 To make the salad, peel and core the pears or *bangkuang* and apples. Slice the apples and sprinkle with lemon juice. Arrange the salad and fruit attractively on a flat platter. The lettuce can be used, instead of a banana leaf, to form a bed for the salad.

4 Add the sliced or quartered hard-boiled eggs (leave quail's eggs whole), the chopped noodles and the Deep-fried Onions.

5 Serve at once, accompanied with a bowl of the Peanut Sauce.

DESSERTS

Desserts do not normally have a high profile on the Indonesian menu; fresh fruit is so abundant that this would be the usual choice after a large buffet meal. However, here is a small sample of favorite dishes. The Deep-fried Bananas are so popular you can buy them from the warungs (street vendors). They are hard to beat when freshly cooked. Do try the Black Glutinous Rice Pudding; it is a unique and delicious experience.

Black Glutinous Rice Pudding

This very unusual rice pudding, *Bubor Pulot Hitam,* which uses bruised fresh ginger root, is quite delicious. When cooked, black rice still retains its husk and has a nutty texture. Serve in small bowls, with a little coconut cream poured over each helping.

INGREDIENTS

Serves 6
4 ounces black glutinous rice
2 cups water
½ inch fresh ginger root, peeled
   and bruised
⅜ cup dark brown sugar
¼ cup superfine sugar
1¼ cups coconut milk
   or cream, to serve

1 Put the rice in a strainer and rinse well under cold running water. Drain and put in a large pan, with the water. Bring to a boil and stir to prevent the rice from settling on the bottom of the pan. Cover and cook for about 30 minutes.

2 Add the ginger and the brown and superfine sugars. Cook for about 15 minutes more, adding a little more water if necessary, until the rice is cooked and like porridge. Remove the ginger and serve warm, in bowls, topped with coconut milk or cream.

Deep-fried Bananas

Known as *Pisang Goreng,* these delicious deep-fried bananas should be cooked at the last minute, so that the outer crust of batter is crisp in texture and the banana is soft and warm inside.

INGREDIENTS

Serves 8
4 ounces self-rising flour
⅜ cup rice flour
½ teaspoon salt
1 cup water
finely grated lime rind (optional)
8 small bananas
oil for deep-frying
sugar and 1 lime, cut in wedges,
   to serve

1 Sift both the flours and the salt together into a bowl. Add just enough water to make a smooth, coating batter. Mix well, then add the lime rind, if using.

2 Peel the bananas and dip them into the batter two or three times.

3 Heat the oil to 375°F or when a cube of day-old bread browns in 30 seconds. Deep-fry the batter-coated bananas until crisp and golden. Drain and serve hot, dredged with sugar and with the lime wedges to squeeze over the bananas.

Pancakes Filled with Sweet Coconut

Traditionally, the pale green color in the batter for *Dadar Gulung* was obtained from the juice squeezed from *pandan* leaves – a real labor of love. Green food coloring can be used as the modern alternative to this lengthy process.

INGREDIENTS

Makes 12–15 pancakes

¾ cup dark brown sugar
2 cups water
1 *pandan* leaf, stripped through with a fork and tied into a knot
6 ounces dried coconut
oil for frying
salt

For the pancake batter
8 ounces flour, sifted
2 eggs, beaten
2 drops edible green food coloring
few drops vanilla extract
scant 2 cups water
3 tablespoons peanut oil

1 Dissolve the sugar in the water with the *pandan* leaf, in a pan over gentle heat, stirring constantly. Increase the heat and allow to boil gently for 3–4 minutes, until the mixture just becomes syrupy. Do not let it caramelize.

2 Put the coconut into a wok with a pinch of salt. Pour over the prepared sugar syrup and cook over a very gentle heat, stirring from time to time, until the mixture becomes almost dry; this will take 5–10 minutes. Set aside until required.

3 To make the batter, blend together the flour, eggs, food coloring, vanilla extract, water and oil either by hand or in a food processor.

4 Brush a 7-inch frying pan with oil and cook 12–15 pancakes. Keep the pancakes warm. Fill each pancake with a generous spoonful of the coconut mixture, roll up and serve them immediately.

Steamed Coconut Custard

Srikaya is a very popular dessert that turns up all over South-east Asia, rather as crème caramel is found all over Europe and the Americas.

INGREDIENTS

Serves 8
14-fluid ounce can coconut milk
5 tablespoons water
1 ounce sugar
3 eggs, beaten
1 ounce cellophane noodles, soaked in warm water for 5 minutes
4 ripe bananas or plantains, peeled and cut in small pieces
salt
vanilla ice cream, to serve (optional)

1 Stir the coconut milk, water and sugar into the beaten eggs and whisk well together.

2 Strain into a 7½-cup heatproof soufflé dish.

3 Drain the noodles well and cut them into small pieces with scissors. Stir the noodles into the coconut milk mixture, together with the chopped bananas or plantains. Stir in a pinch of salt.

4 Cover the dish with foil and place in a steamer for about 1 hour, or until set. Test by inserting a thin, small knife or skewer into the center. Serve hot or cold, on its own or topped with vanilla ice cream.

Index

Apples: carrot and apple salad, 64
Aromatic chicken from Madura, 48

Balinese spiced duck, 52
Balinese vegetable soup, 29
Bamie goreng, 77
Bananas: deep-fried bananas, 92
    steamed coconut custard, 95
Barbecued pork spareribs, 50
Bean curd and cucumber salad, 84
Beef: beef and eggplant curry, 57
    clear soup with meatballs, 16
    nasi goreng, 73
    noodles with meatballs, 76
    omelets with spicy meat
        filling, 18
    rendang, 44
    spiced beef satés, 26
    spicy meat fritters, 50
    spicy meat patties with
        coconut, 14
    spicy meat-filled packages, 20
    spicy meatballs, 56
    vegetable broth with ground
        beef, 18
Black glutinous rice pudding, 92
Boemboe Bali of fish, 39

Cabbage: cooked vegetable gado-
    gado, 88
Carrot and apple salad, 64
Cauliflower: spiced cauliflower
    braise, 80
Chayote: shrimp with chayote in
    turmeric sauce, 36
Chicken: aromatic chicken from
    Madura, 48
    bamie goreng, 77
    chicken cooked in coconut
        milk, 47
    chicken with spices and soy
        sauce, 49
    chicken with turmeric, 46
    grilled chicken, 45
    nasi goreng, 73
    rice porridge with chicken, 74
    sambal goreng, 62
    spiced chicken sauté 54
    spiced vegetable soup with
        chicken and shrimp, 26
    stir-fried chicken with
        pineapple, 54
    stir-fried greens, 85
Chili crabs, 38
Chili sambal, 66
Chinese cabbage: bamie goreng, 77
    fruit and raw vegetable gado-
        gado, 89
    spicy scrambled eggs, 80
    stir-fried greens, 85
Coconut: chicken cooked in
    coconut milk, 47
    coconut and peanut relish, 82
    coconut rice, 74
    pancakes filled with sweet
        coconut, 94
    spicy meat patties with
        coconut, 14
    steamed coconut custard, 95
Cod: boemboe Bali of fish, 39
Corn: spicy scrambled eggs, 80

corn fritters, 14
Crab: chili crabs, 38
Cucumber: bean curd and
    cucumber salad, 84
    sweet and sour fruit and
        vegetable salad, 66

Deep-fried onions, 60
Deep-fried wonton pillows with
    sambal kecap, 28
Doedoeh of fish, 36
Duck: Balinese spiced duck, 52
    duck with Chinese mushrooms
        and ginger, 53

Eggplant: beef and eggplant
    curry, 57
Eggs: bamie goreng, 77
    cooked vegetable gado-
        gado, 88
    egg sambal goreng, 62
    fruit and raw vegetable gado-
        gado, 89
    nasi goreng, 73
    omelets with spicy meat
        filling, 18
    spicy scrambled eggs, 80

Festive rice, 72
Filo pastry: spicy meat-filled
    packages, 20
Fish: boemboe Bali of fish, 39
    doedoeh of fish, 36
    spiced whole fish, baked or
        grilled, 40
    spicy fish, 32
    vinegar fish, 40
    whole fish with sweet and sour
        sauce, 34
Fritters: corn fritters, 14
    peanut fritters, 22
    spicy meat fritters, 50
Fruit: fruit and raw vegetable gado-
    gado, 89
    sweet and sour fruit and
        vegetable salad, 66

Gado-gado: cooked vegetable gado-
    gado, 88
    fruit and raw vegetable gado-
        gado, 89
Grilled chicken, 45

Indonesian potatoes with onions
    and chili sauce, 86

Kroepoek, 22

Lamb satés, 24

Madura, aromatic chicken from, 48
Mixed vegetable pickle, 63
Mushrooms: clear soup with
    meatballs, 16
    duck with Chinese mushrooms
        and ginger, 53

Nasi goreng, 73
Noodles: bamie goreng, 77
    noodles, chicken and shrimp in
        coconut broth, 70

fruit and raw vegetable gado-
    gado, 89
noodles, chicken and shrimp in
    coconut broth, 70
noodles with meatballs, 76
zucchini with noodles, 86

Omelet: festive rice, 72
    nasi goreng, 73
    omelets with spicy meat
        filling, 18
Onions: deep-fried onions, 60
    Indonesian potatoes with onions
        and chili sauce, 86
    tomato and onion salad, 82

Pancakes filled with sweet
    coconut, 94
Peanuts: coconut and peanut
    relish, 82
    peanut fritters, 22
    peanut sauce, 89
    tamarind soup with peanuts and
        vegetables, 17
Pickles and relishes: coconut and
    peanut relish, 82
    mixed vegetable pickle, 63
Pineapple: fruit and raw vegetable
    gado-gado, 89
    stir-fried chicken with
        pineapple, 54
Pork: bamie goreng, 77
    barbecued pork spareribs, 50
    deep-fried wonton pillows with
        sambal kecap, 28
    nasi goreng, 73
    pork satés, 21
    stir-fried greens, 85
Potatoes: cooked vegetable gado-
    gado, 88
    Indonesian potatoes with onions
        and chili sauce, 86
    spicy meat fritters, 50

Quail's eggs: fruit and raw vegetable
    gado-gado, 89
    stir-fried greens, 85

Rendang, 44
Rice: black glutinous rice
    pudding, 92
    coconut rice, 74
    compressed-rice shapes, 70
    festive rice, 72
    nasi goreng, 73
    rice porridge with chicken, 74
Salad: bean curd and cucumber
    salad, 84
    carrot and apple salad, 64
    sweet and sour fruit and
        vegetable salad, 66
    tomato and onion salad, 82
Sambals: chili sambal, 66
    sambal goreng, 62
    sambal kecap, 60
    tomato sambal, 64
Satés: lamb satés, 24
    pork satés, 21
    shrimp satés, 25
    spiced beef satés, 26

Shrimp: bamie goreng, 77
    deep-fried wonton pillows with
        sambal kecap, 28
    nasi goreng, 73
    shrimp crackers, 22
    shrimp sambal goreng, 62
    shrimp satés, 25
    shrimp with chayote in turmeric
        sauce, 36
    spiced vegetable soup with
        chicken and shrimp, 26
Spiced beef satés, 26
Spiced cauliflower braise, 80
Spiced chicken sauté, 54
Spiced vegetable soup with chicken
    and shrimp, 26
Spiced whole fish, baked or
    grilled, 40
Spicy fish, 32
Spicy meat-filled packages, 20
Spicy meat fritters, 50
Spicy meat patties with coconut, 14
Spicy meatballs, 56
Spicy scrambled eggs, 80
Spicy squid, 35
Spinach: cooked vegetable gado-
    gado, 88
    stir-fried greens, 85
Squid: spicy squid, 35
    squid from Madura, 32
Steamed coconut custard, 95
Stir-fried chicken with
    pineapple, 54
Stir-fried greens, 85

Tamarind: doedoeh of fish, 36
    tamarind soup with peanuts and
        vegetables, 17
Tomatoes: fruit and raw vegetable
    gado-gado, 89
    tomato and onion salad, 82
    tomato sambal goreng, 62
    tomato sambal, 64
Turmeric: chicken with
    turmeric, 46
    mixed vegetable pickle, 63
    shrimp with chayote in turmeric
        sauce, 36

Vegetables: Balinese vegetable
    soup, 29
    cooked vegetable gado-gado, 88
    fruit and raw vegetable gado-
        gado, 89
    mixed vegetable pickle, 63
    spiced vegetable soup with
        chicken and shrimp, 26
    stir-fried greens, 85
    sweet and sour fruit and
        vegetable salad, 66
    tamarind soup with peanuts and
        vegetables, 17
Vinegar fish, 40

Whole fish with sweet and sour
    sauce, 34
Wontons: deep-fried wonton
    pillows with sambal
    kecap, 28

Zucchini with noodles, 86